"Hope springs eternal for the au

who blows into San Francisco in 1977 at the age of 21 and sees romantic possibility in every denim bulge, every cruisy glance, every trail of kisses that leads to bed. A literate and literary observer, he unapologetically guides the reader—squirt by squirt—through a tempestuous era, surviving fire, earthquake, plague, psychotic boyfriends, and other natural disasters with humor and libido intact. I was moved to find an entire emotional life crammed into these pages: loss, love, fear, doubt, joy."
—Don Shewey, author of *Sam Shepard*, contributor to *Best Gay Erotica 2000*

"Very moving and also very unusual, these exciting diaries are filled with warmth, humor, San Francisco history, and the fascination of an honest and courageous life."
—Jerry Rosco, author of *Glenway Wescott Personally*

"*Wild Animals I Have Known* is terrific reading. I sped through it, envying the author both his wild experiences and his ability to describe them. His writing is direct, intelligent, savagely funny, and very, very erotic—and all the more arresting (and arousing) for its vivid, unvarnished reality. He evokes brilliantly a lost world, a San Francisco bursting with reckless pleasures and dangers."
—Kevin Dax, author of *D.O.C.: Lust Letters*

Wild Animals I Have Known

I Have Known

Polk Street Diaries and After

Wild Animals I Have Known
Polk Street Diaries and After

Kevin Bentley

Green Candy Press

Wild Animals I Have Known: Polk Street Diaries and After
by Kevin Bentley
ISBN 1-931160-08-2

Published by Green Candy Press
www.greencandypress.com

Cover and interior design: Ian Phillips
Front cover photo: Crawford Barton, courtesy
GLBT Historical Society of Northern California

Some proper names and details have been changed in the
following autobiographical account to protect the privacy of
living individuals.

The entries beginning with March 3, 1996 and ending with
November 30, 1996 first appeared as "Reasons to Live" in
Afterwords: Real Sex from Gay Men's Diaries, published by
Alyson Books.

Printed in Canada by Transcontinental Printing Inc.
Massively Distributed by P.G.W.

For Cora McClure

We come to you as from the dead. The things about which you ask us have been dead to us for many years. In bringing them to our minds we are calling them from the dead, and when we have told you about them they will go back to the dead, to remain forever.—Moses Old Bull

1977

August 13, 1977

Every boy or girl must make a break and leave home sooner or later, and if he or she is gay, it's probably sooner and a bit further. One day I was finishing up summer session courses and dreading student teaching in the fall, and the next I was following the black Magic Markered route on a series of creased highway maps to San Francisco in a red, '69 VW with my worldly possessions in the back seat and $500 in Traveler's Checks in my sock. My crime? I'd met a man at the Pet Shop and stayed out all night, again.

"Maybe you'll be happy where there are others like you," Mom said, wiping her eyes.

"Queer! Fairy! Faggot!" said Dad.

When the attendant at a filling station in Needles glanced at my Texas license plates and asked with a wink if it was true *everything* in Texas is bigger, I knew I was headed in the right direction.

That was three weeks ago. Now here I am in my *Planet of the Apes* red polyester tunic with the little cat-eared, pointy-breasted silhouette dancing on the shoulder patch, balancing my notebook behind the popcorn machine at the concession counter I operate 5:30 to 2:30 A.M. five nights a week here at the Pussycat Erotic Theater on Market Street. Last week I walked all over downtown leaving resumés first at bookstores, then trying anything. Stuart, the evil leather queen manager here, called right away. ("I'm going to take a chance on you, Kevin," he said sternly, looking me up and down. You'd think I was applying to the naval academy.) Three years of English lit, history, and creative writing have more than qualified me for serving up stale popcorn, flat soda, and petrified hot dogs to a very odd assortment of patrons and answering the constantly ringing phone to say, "That's right, tonight's three-hour features are *Oriental Babysitter* and *Sticky Fingers.*" Most of the callers are creeps who wait for the spiel and then say something like, "You know what? I'm coming down there and I'm going to cut your prick off and feed it to you." Just a moment, sir, you must be looking for Stuart.

But I'm lucky to have found something without having to quite stoop to fast food. I've only glimpsed the flicks themselves; they're straight, though my colleagues mostly are not. What I saw made me disinclined to see more: western music was playing and a cowgirl was shitting into a cowboy hat. Huh? I feel I've definitely jumped in at the deep end; I stand here for hours watching the most bizarre parade of people out of a Max Fleisher cartoon cavorting past the blinking light bulbs that frame the lobby.

I punch a broken antique cash register behind this joke concession stand (on which the keys are so greasy it's hard to hit them effectively), tear tickets at the door and shoot the breeze with an eighty-year-old cashier named Sadie Blumenthal who says she's been selling tickets since silent films. She's the perky kind; says things like "I'm just as young as any of these kids, I tell you!" and punctuates her remarks with a little Charleston shuffle and kick. There're a couple of other gay clone guys who're unaccountably unfriendly, as if I might threaten their seniority here at the Pussycat Academy.

As I write I'm stopping to ring up drinks ("I'd like a diet Pepsi and a Coke, please." "Sorry, all we have is this grape stuff.") or flashlight people to their seats (shadowy figures scrambling to a sitting position as the thin beam hits them. The porn may be straight, but my impression is that basically scary people are back there sucking off even scarier people in the murky darkness). Our hottest item at the concession stand is napkins; most people grab a handful on their way in, without stopping for a delicious snack.

This, for now, is the price of my ticket to stay here in Disneyland and walk among the painted dollhouses, rumbling green streetcars, mustached men with shocking bulges in their crotches, and the chilling, unreal daily fog that blunts sound like a mattress.

September 18, 1977

I went with Buddy and Fred to see Ted Hughes read on August 7 at the Museum of Modern Art. He looks now like one of the illustrations by Leonard Baskin in *Crow*, from which he mostly read. Reading "Heptonstall Cemetery" he intoned a series of names on the tombstones; when he reached "Sylvia," an excited murmuring swept the audience. But the biggest excitement came just as he walked up to the mike and opened his mouth to begin. The double doors at the back of the auditorium burst open and smacked the wall with a loud bang and the crazed, presumably estranged boyfriend of a long-black-skirted, pony-tailed girl in the audience ran down the aisle ripping pages from a book and screaming at her as she stood and wrung her hands, "You Sylvia Plath whore! Sylvia Plath bitch!" An elderly British woman seated behind us rapped on the floor with her cane and shouted, "Call a constable!" Security guards dragged him back down the aisle, still yelling abuse, and out the doors, and Ted, unsmiling, cleared his throat and began to read without comment.

I've been fucking around a lot since I got here, but no real boyfriend as yet. When I first arrived in mid-July, I was taken straight into bed by my new roommates, Buddy and Fred. Buddy and I'd done it plenty back in El Paso; Fred's the lover he's moved out here from Austin with and now seems to be leaving. A friend of a co-worker at the Pussycat came home with me but annoyed me by giving me a pedantic lecture on how to give a proper blowjob. He was my first professional clone: big, half-tumescent dick arrayed just so in his jeans, keys to nowhere, as Buddy and I like to say, jangling on his left hip, and that pathetic colored hanky thing (which always reminds me of Western Day in grade school).

A few days before giving my notice at the Pussycat (upon which I was angrily informed by Stuart, whose nose and upper lip were inflamed from a mishap with a bottle of poppers, that I'd never work for Pussycat Corporation again, *ever*), I walked home at 3:30 A.M. with Johnny, the muscular, gap-toothed, married Puerto Rican guy with whom I'd been working my shift. He talked about fucking women all the way back to the Noe Street flat, as we passed a bottle of red wine back and forth and smoked a tiny joint of doubtful content he'd provided—then, back in my narrow room next to the airshaft, I sucked his purple-headed, funky uncut dick while he slugged at the warm wine and mumbled about "popping cherries." The next day I got the phone call from Mrs. Eidenmueller, owner of the large, forty-year-old bookstore with the black awnings out front next to Crocker Plaza: "The position is yours, if you want it."

For the last several weeks I've been seeing Jim, a thirty-four-year-old Burt Reynolds look-alike with a silver burr who likes to smoke pot, drink, and take acid; who acts a total butch role but once in bed wants only to be fucked by me. He has a tiny, snarling, fluffy dog named Greta who snaps at me, and who has invariably deposited a puddle of runny shit on the shag just inside the door when Jim and I come back to his place, not a thing one can encounter on LSD and ever really be quite the same again.

November 27, 1977

Wednesday night I went out with Steve, an older (thirty-one) gay clerk at Bonanza Books with whom I've been hanging out since my roommate situation unraveled at the end of last month and I moved to my own place in this Victorian pile on Pine Street. We sat around my studio drinking Wide-Mouth Mickeys and talking, then went to the 'N Touch and danced on that ridiculous, blinking, ten by ten disco floor that looks like the set of some game show.

I slipped out two hours later while Steve was dancing with a very cute boy with a blond Prince Valiant, with whom he seemed likely to leave, trudged up Pine Street, and went to bed without troubling to undress. And so woke with a hangover for Thanksgiving, and set to peeling a dozen avocados for a giant bowl of guacamole, my ill-conceived contribution to the spread at a party I was attending with new boyfriend Nick and his phony friend Audrey ("Audree" is how she spells it, actually, on the autographed publicity still framed on his mantel—

"all my love…"—she's a lounge singer without a lounge, as far as I can tell, and his main buddy from est training, so there's always lots of wise nodding and fractured aphorisms when they're together). The guac turned black and went untouched.

Nick, met on a Saturday night in early October at last call at the Elephant Walk: he's a big, shaggy-haired, thirty-seven-year-old psychologist with a little house in Noe Valley. He took mushrooms at the Thanksgiving party; I abstained. Back at his place that night, I really got into blowing him—he was very excited, his dick red and hard and thrusting. "Wow, handsome, what's got into you?" he said, after I'd swallowed his cum and shot my own wad.

I left work with Steve again the following day and took a Jackson bus to his dark and bare little studio on Pine at Leavenworth (beat-up brown leather bomber jacket he wears to the bars hanging on the back of the door, mattress on the creaking, uneven, water-stained hardwood floor, pile of French paperbacks) so he could change shirts and call a friend who might have some acid. Just thinking about taking it had me feeling jumpy before we'd left the store: Mrs. E. glared at us from behind her wood-panel and leaded-glass antique office façade, thinking, no doubt, *Kevin and Steve leaving together, hmmm.* Or had I left *The Joy of Gay Sex* out on the new arrivals table too long before censoring it to the cook-book corner?

We walked to Polk Street, which was already teeming with hustlers and cruisers and crazies, bought a six-pack, and went to my place at Pine and Franklin to drink till time to meet the guy with the acid at The Wild Goose. As usual, Steve did most of the talking, sitting in my green vinyl office chair from Goodwill, while I propped myself on the yellow Cost Plus Indian spread-covered mattress. I was getting drunk and staring at Steve's Dutch Boy profile (the upturned nose, the light brown mop of sixties pop singer hair), backlit by a yellow bar of light from the half-shut bathroom door. I'm still quite smitten with him, though my designated role is clearly that of sidekick. He thinks I'm wasting my time with Nick. "Let me guess, you suck his dick or he fucks you, and then he smokes a cigarette while you jack off," he said meanly, but fairly accurately.

"Sometimes he sucks me," I said. He has, two or three times.

"Till you come? Ever?"

"OK, OK," I said. "The selfish thing can be exciting. You're living proof of that."

"You need more drugs," Steve said, and we both pissed like racehorses, and headed back down to Polk to meet the Acid Man.

Saturday morning, still half-tripping, I called Nick, who was "painting" in the greenhouse room at the back of his house. I took the streetcar to Castro and walked up the hill and over; found Nick daubing at a splotchy, impressionistic rendering of a weed he'd spotted at his Marin County retreat. He was wearing loose gym shorts, and I hugged and groped him till he asked if I wanted to go upstairs and fuck. His dick was hard and he palmed some Vaseline onto it and pushed it up my ass, my legs over his shoulders, and fucked me till he came. After a brief nap, I woke and beat off sucking his dick, and when he flooded my mouth with a second, bitter load, I shot so hard—between the leftover acid and having my ass plowed—I hit the oak headboard and my chin.

December 4, 1977
I woke in the very early hours on Wednesday to the noisy clanging of this run-down building's fire alarm, panicky yelling in the hall outside my door, running footsteps and shouted instructions. I leapt out of bed (mattress on the floor) and yanked on boots and shirt and ran out. The cute blond English-accented straight boy from the next floor was dashing by with a dysfunctional fire extinguisher, yelling "Bloody fucking place, this's too much, we're fuckin' getting out of here!" Out on the street my till now mostly unseen neighbors milled about in comic undress loaded with cameras, electric mixers, easels and portfolios. I hadn't even grabbed a coat, and stood shivering beside Danielle, the pretty, coffee-colored

black girl who lives with the British boy; she seemed to be wearing nothing but a fur coat, which was rather glamorous. Would the scene have been complete without the thin older lady in a hairnet and bathrobe cradling a fat cat? Two fire engines pulled up, sirens yowling, radios crackling. I never glimpsed the flames or smoke; word is that a wall went up in flames in an empty studio on the floor above me. And no one owns to having pulled the alarm. To top off the B-movie plot, the spooky Section Eight guy from downstairs was walking around saying, "It wasn't me, nope, I wasn't anywhere near that floor," and we all simultaneously looked at him and then each other as if it were choreographed.

Nick, ever the middle-school psychologist, says if I have any sense of self-value I should come and stay at his house till this is solved.

Friday night I was sitting in a hot bath hoping Nick might call; the phone rang, but it was Steve. He'd been crowing at work for the last two days about the handsome bartender at Buzby's who'd come right up to him on Wednesday night and asked him out for dinner on Friday. "I could really use a good affair with the right person," Steve had said, puffing a cigarette in the shipping room while customers tapped at the door and asked, "You got that police exam test book?" "Try Stacey's." But they jumped the gun and got together Thursday night at Steve's and had nasty, reciprocal sex—they both got fucked. "I'm in love," he said the next day, making little kiss-kiss lips. "I'm all goo-gooey." It's all I heard about Friday. "I'm so horny, I just can't wait to see him again."

But when he called me at nine—"Uh, yeah, Steve,"—the dream fuck had rudely stood him up. "I'm OK," he said. "It's just *so* San Francisco."

December 11, 1977

Last Monday night I went to Steve's for spaghetti, then went to meet friends of his from Monterey in the Haight to buy some MDM. We swallowed capsules, bussed back to Polk Street, and went drinking at Kimo's and Buzby's. Just when I was really high and feeling amorous toward Steve, he took off with a slim, blond, khaki-panted Jewish boy named Reuben, who carried a bottle of prescribed Quaaludes fetchingly in his back pocket.

The next day, Tuesday, Steve was very horny and flirtatious with me at work, asked if I'd like to get together later for potato pancakes and sour cream, and two more hits of MDM. I hadn't been able to bathe that morning, as there wasn't any hot water, so after we'd picked up and downed the capsules at Steve's, shopped at Cala Market (where I started to get fucked up; Steve had to drag me away from a refrigerater bin where I was mesmerized by the painting on a Land O' Lakes butter package), and made our way to my studio, I found the water

working and filled a tub while he opened beers and began dinner. Of course I got really stoned in my steamy bath, Steve
cranking up David Bowie's "Station to Station" in the next
room, and I emerged in a towel to find a thick white halluci-
natory fog pervading the other two rooms (some of it the
result of a failed attempt at cooking), Steve grinning mania-
cally and meeting my gaze, laughing and stepping toward me.
Then it was as if everything had been planned to lead to this:
we were kissing passionately and grabbing each other's dicks.
We played on and off for hours, sucking each other, kissing
long and studiously—he's got such plump, red lips; Steve
screwing me, me screwing him. We took a tranquilizer each
with a beer as we began to come down, and he passed out and
I lay admiring his still body, then I was hard again and rolling
him over and pushing my cock back up inside him, and he was
moaning and moving back against me in his sleep. We woke
horny at five and I fucked him again, then he pinned me down
and fucked me for so long I couldn't take it anymore, and
instead sucked him off till he shot. As he dressed to leave Steve
said, just as he had the first time we made love, "This may not
happen again for a long time."

December 13, 1977
Last night after work Steve came by here to eat tuna sandwiches and finish off the Zinfandel I'd bought for dinner with

Nick last week. We smoked several joints and drank up the wine talking non-stop. Next thing I knew we had stopped talking and were just smiling and high—and then we lunged at each other and fell onto the mattress dragging each other's pants and underwear down and 69'd till we came almost simultaneously. There's no doubt I'm exceedingly hot for Steve—those juicy lips and the way he kisses, his thick, tasty uncircumcised cock; I think of them as being made of the same stuff.

"You know, I really like you a lot. I mean, I really do," he says.

1978

January 2, 1978

One day last week The Amazing Kreskin walked into the store to sign the three copies of his mind power book we (luckily) had stacked on the front table. He was immediately recognizable from all the times I saw him on Johnny Carson when I was a child; in person, the most amazing thing about him was how stunningly ugly he was. Steve swore that Kreskin had looked into Mrs. E.'s mind as they spoke and left abruptly with a pained look on his face.

New Year's Eve I was walking up Pine with the little black and white TV I'd just bought in my arms when I spotted the sexiest of my three straight upstairs building-mates slouching along. After jointly refusing admittance to a group of Jehovah's Witness ladies at the front door on our way in, we got to talking, and I asked him up to smoke a joint. He's swarthy, short, thick-lipped, wide-eyed, and talks in this sexy, hushed, confidential tone. Just as we were chummily passing a joint and comparing notes on our religious upbringings (mine Baptist, his Catholic), the phone rang: Nick. I'd agreed the day before to accompany him to a gym he's just joined, but now, high and flirting with the swarthy one, I couldn't be bothered.

He wanted to go into my defection at length; I cut him short. He called back a few minutes later: "I just want you to know I'm really pissed about this." "OK," I said.

He called again later. "I'm going to be in your neighborhood and I'd like to pick up my records and give you back your Vaseline," he said, icily. "Um, OK," I said. I'd made plans to go out with Steve.

When he arrived I handed him the couple of albums he'd lent me, and stood inanely drying a Melitta filter with a dirty dishtowel. He looked grim, purse-lipped, and fat. "I haven't seen any of the things in you these last few weeks that initially attracted me."

How many times were we going to break up? I thought we already had. "If you mean I'm not your doting little boy anymore, no, I guess that's changed."

"You've done a pretty good job of killing all that off."

What's the good of letting your hair grow out if you can't toss it? I tossed. "Whatever you say, Nick."

He gave me a hug, for which I stayed noncommittally rigid, arms at my sides, and then backed to the door, which he couldn't get open for a moment—awkward seconds while he struggled with the loose doorknob—and then he was gone. I had thrown in my lot with single adventure.

Steve tapped at the door so soon after, they must surely have passed on the stairs.

January 23, 1978

I went with Steve to the Liberty Baths on Post Street on Friday night. We wandered together at first, and began making out in a little cul-de-sac where I fucked him while men gathered around to watch, stroke, and masturbate, then I found my way into a dark padded sort of bunkhouse enclosure where I enjoyed my first six-way, sucking off two nice cocks whose owners I could barely distinguish in the jumble of legs, arms, buttocks, and mouths. I was sucked off twice, and was headed to the lockers thinking I was all finished when a sweet, handsome older man coaxed me back to his room. We made out awhile and he blew me, then he fucked me slowly for a very long time with an unusually thick circumcised dick. "You should come back to New York with me and be my lover. No, I'm serious. I'd fuck you like this every day; that's what you need. Wouldn't you like to fly back to New York and live with me?" (Steve had advised me not to tell anyone my real name or give out my number.) I slept for a while in daddy's arms, then kissed him good-bye, showered, and walked home in a sort of exhausted ecstasy at 4:00 A.M.

Last Tuesday night I brought a man named Joaquin home from the 'N Touch—a sort of tall, skinny, hippie type—and fucked him sitting astride my cock in the bathtub. I'd just shot inside him and was jerking off his hard, red dick when, above the cranked-up stereo, we heard a rush of heavy footsteps on the stairs outside my door. I dripped my way to the door in a towel to check it out, and found a flock of black-coated firemen racing up and down the stairs, hose trailing, several of them hefting a smoldering sofa out—another arson attempt, apparently. One of the very hunky firemen stopped and eyed me appraisingly, wet and panting in my towel, Joaquin peering naked from the bathroom. "No reason to leave now, the fire's out. Don't you two have any clothes?"

June 12, 1978

Last Saturday night Steve and I went to a dinner party at George Hammersmith's. Hammersmith is this sixty-year-old, cricket-like, pretentious, fake-British-accented, trust-fund queen who's shopped at Bonanza forever, comes in and checks out the new talent, inquires imperiously about expensive books on royalty and then buys $1.98 books from the remainder tables. He's funny, though, and we were curious to see what kind of flat he has, and figured we'd get a good meal and drinks out of it. Of course Steve turned up with hits of blue dot acid and we were already so fucked up we couldn't find the apartment number when we reached the block it was on, and Hammersmith had to yell down to us from a window.

There was a crew of much older queens sitting around the living room with big cocktails sweating into knitted coasters. It looked like the poker game in *Sunset Boulevard*. Our host was hardly recognizable out of his usual faux-English-gentle-man suit and vest; instead he wore tight black slacks and a shiny black shirt—and a belt with a buckle that appeared to be a laughing skull.

We were given shots of Stoly with something horrible like Worcester sauce and black pepper, which made me sneeze and feel queasy. A plump silver-haired man sat down beside me on the couch and patted my leg with a damp hand. "So, you're a new arrival to our *wicked* city! We must certainly corrupt you straight away." It was like being leered at by Alistair Cooke. I was madly looking around for Steve, who'd started dropping French vocabulary into his conversation and wandered off. After several more Stolys and some very awkward conversation ("Don't you think that *pain* and *pleasure* are sometimes very similar sensations?"), I excused myself to go looking for the bathroom, and when I noticed the street door, I made one of those very high, self-preserving, split-second decisions and bailed, coatless. I was somewhere in Pacific Heights. I had even less sense of direction than I do when sober, so I had to walk a very long way in the wrong direction before I discovered my mistake and turned back toward Polk Street. When I reached my faded yellow apartment building on Post (relocated to in February), the usual shrieking fire engine was pulling out of the station directly across the street as I tried to fit the right key in the door while hallucinating to a degree that would have been enjoyable if it hadn't made getting home such a task.

July 16, 1978

I have reached a diminishing rate of installments: month to month, to nothing at all. I wrote "I married nothing" in one of my star turns at the poetry workshop on Thursday nights down at Marina High, inspired by my torrid affair with the workshop teacher, who already had a lover but claimed to be passionately in love with me for a month and gave me rides home to bed and gonorrhea to prove it. The line was apt, if not original: months before, Gina, a strange, soft-spoken girl with a fox-like nose and big, liquid eyes, who also attends the workshop, read aloud a poem with the line, "And I am mother to nothing." She and I seem to have nothing in common.

Last night, Saturday, I did acid with Steve and his est-graduate boyfriend Chuck. Chuck had just come home with the new Rolling Stones album and we came on to the drug lying on the bed listening to "Miss You," the beat and hooting refrain of which became the backdrop of the evening. I didn't do my usual bolt till 1:30 A.M., after we'd wobbled out of Chuck's Pacific Heights apartment, hiked up Alta Plaza Park to view the blinking city lights, then stumbled wide-eyed and incoherent into The Lion, where I took one look at the gauntlet of staring men beneath the framed drawing of a nude clone in crew socks being sodomized by a lion, realized I was too high to talk to strangers, and fled.

September 30, 1978
Steve's moved back to Monterey and I'm pissed at him. He quit Bonanza and moved in with me (strictly roommates) on Post Street, then went to bartender school and started tending bar at a dive called Googie's on Geary. We rented this bigger place together on Bush Street, then he tricked with a boozy couple he met at the bar and left me high and dry for a three-way living arrangement with them. I had to hustle to find a replacement roommate; I found Dave, a blond waiter my age who I almost never see, through roommate listings. Then Steve called to say the three-way hadn't worked out and he's returned to Monterey and is working as a waiter again there.

I've been having a smutty, purely physical thing with a Jewish bi-sexual named Leslie Green. He's very intellectual, or at least feigns to be so; works as a copywriter but claims to be a writer, talks too much about D. H. Lawrence. He's got a fiancée, Sandra, likes to talk about getting me together with the two of them for sex: he'd like to fuck me while I fuck her—but this is all fantasy; I don't think she knows of his homosexual activities.

I met him at the Cinch one Friday night. The sex is reciprocal to a degree; he sucks me off and lets me fuck him some of the time—but he's very stern, smug, and bossy, almost bullying. He's got pale skin, jet-black hair, inky five o'clock shadow, big nose, dorky black-framed glasses. He's got a burly torso, biceps, and kinky black hair all over. There's something very pornographic about him; he looks more naked than other people do when he's stripped, and he's very unsmiling and serious about sex. His dick is usually bone-hard from the moment I see it. He's rough when he fucks, and it's not that his cock's so large but that it's always so hard and he jabs so brutally with it. Sucking him is exciting because it's sort of repugnant at the same time; he stares at me and makes me look up at him while I'm blowing him, and that hard dick has a bitter, waxy taste, ditto his cum, which he's insistent about my swallowing.

I went over to his apartment on Nob Hill one night a couple weeks ago; he came to the door in an old white terry-cloth robe and leather slippers, smoking his pipe. He offered me a beer and we sat talking a few minutes. He sat with his legs apart, and very shortly the robe had fallen open enough for his pale boner to jut out. Then I was between his legs and sucking, while he went on puffing at his pipe, pushing my head down and jamming his cock down my throat till he shot his bitter load there.

Last week I met him for *The Lords of Flatbush* at the Strand on my weekday off. We came back here—Dave was at work—and smoked a joint and started messing around down on the shag carpet. We shoved our pants and underwear down far enough to get at each other's dicks and took turns blowing each other. I rimmed his hairy ass and he reached for my dick and said to put it in. This was the best fuck I've had with him—his legs were tangled up in his pants, his Jockey shorts yanked down to his knees, and his asshole was dry and tight. I fucked him hard and fast and shot my brains out, then lay panting on top of him, my dick still clamped inside him. Now if I know I'm going to be getting fucked, I hold off coming; I need that full-on urge to take a cock. Leslie pushed me off and rolled over; of course his dick was red and throbbing. "Now your turn." I wasn't aroused again yet, I wasn't sure I was up to it, but he wasn't having any excuses. I rolled over reluctantly and submitted, my fists clenched under my chest as he jabbed that torpedo cock into me with a little saliva and fucked me so frantically I thought surely I'd be bleeding when he was done. It was as if he was pissed off with me for fucking him and was now getting even, though I'd only done as he asked.

October 25, 1978
I've met another sexy Jewish guy, this one a thirty-nine-year-old curly-haired blond with a very acerbic wit and more sneering comic voices than Mel Blanc. Frank's a divorced, out of work advertising director from New York, sophisticated and quite stuck-up, but very charming. He's a total top in

bed, at least with me. The first night we went home together he wanted me to strip naked and stand across the room jacking off in front of a mirror; then I had to bend over and spread my cheeks like I was getting a physical, while he sat on the couch in his underwear, his erection poking up and making a wet spot. I'm totally smitten with him; we've gone on seeing each other pretty regularly for several weeks now, but I can see he doesn't consider me lover material. He's thrilled to be fucking a twenty-two-year-old, physically, but also teases me evilly about being a hick from Texas. When I objected indignantly once that all my other friends seem to think I'm pretty intelligent, he put on a sort of Cookie Monster voice to represent these friends and growled, "Ohhh Kevin, you *so* smart!"

1979

March 15, 1979

It's been six weeks now since I stormed out of Frank's place "to find someone who *did* want to make love with me." We'd progressed from intense first weeks to being vague fuck buddies, to grudging meetings on his part. I was in love with him, but he tired of the novelty of sex with a raw youth, and never really entertained the idea of anything more serious between us. "You're still just a baby," he said more than once.

I was bewailing the latest downturn in my love life to Bob Mainardi at work. He's the gay guy, Steve's age, who used to be paperback buyer at the store in *his* twenties, and who still comes in one day a week to stock the remainders. He and his partner run a vintage magazine and used smut shop. Bob said, "If it's any comfort to you, I didn't even *begin* to be happy till after I was thirty."

As I walked home from the Castro the other night the air reeked of coming rain, and there were wafts from budding trees when I passed the monumental Civic Center buildings. I saw groups of sailors in their absurd white uniforms clustered at the fringes of Polk Street when I passed that way. Were they there to gawk at the fabled San Francisco queers, or hoping to meet some?

April 12, 1979

I ran into Michael Harper on Polk Street one night last week. I've seen him around since meeting him briefly when he tricked with Steve a few times about a year and a half ago: he's a short, shaggy-blond-haired boy, has been on Polk since his teens, comes from a carnival family and is full of stories. He's like a debauched Partridge Family member—looks sixteen (I think he's nineteen) and squeaky-clean, with a touch of baby fat—streetwise, but somehow not quite a hustler or at least not anymore, and very funny. He invited himself home to spend the night with me, and to my surprise started grabbing my dick when we got into bed (I hadn't thought he'd be interested in me sexually). He has these albino-looking white eyelashes, a light down of white-blond hair all over his body, including on his plump, round little ass, which I got to stick my dick in. He talked a steady stream of fantasy while I fucked him: coach and jock in the locker room, tenderfoot and eagle scout in a tent; I came just as the gang rape was getting under way on cell block one.

"There," he said brightly as we showered together afterward, "now we can be friends."

June 1, 1979

Last Sunday I went to the Haight Street Fair with Nate, the new gay boy at the bookstore who's become a pal. There are places in this city where 1967 never ended, and this was one:

there were lots of shirtless guys with glitter in their hair and painted nipples, the air was heavy with patchouli and pot. We were smoking joints and drinking beer as we wandered up and down the crowded, debris-strewn blocks. When the fog rolled in we rolled into some jammed bar to pee and I quickly lost sight of Nate. I was drunk and stoned and it didn't seem to be a gay bar, but I couldn't really tell; here, and out in the parade crush, there were just sexy guys who didn't seem to mind being stared at, and many of them were looking back.

I was standing near a wall with a beer listening to deafening rock and roll when I met the eye of a hot guy, my age or only slightly older, who I'd noticed standing a few feet away in the crowd: longish light brown hair, sinewy Mick Jagger build, rumpled white jeans and bowling shirt. He looked like a hip straight boy from my high school days, and I assumed he *was* straight and looked away. A few minutes later he'd moved closer to stand beside me, his shoulder crowding mine. This was all happening in the midst of a seething crowd lashed by high-decibel 60s rock; I was very high and certainly freer of inhibitions than normally. I turned to look at him and he simply pushed me with both hands on my shoulders back against what I'd taken for a wall, and instead a door edged open to an enclosed storage alley piled high with boxes of beer, and we tumbled through.

Next I was standing pushed up against an outer wall in the narrow space and we were making out frantically. He had a large mouth and full, rubbery lips and intelligent eyes and he was holding the sides of my head and jamming his tongue down my throat. Why can't it always be like this—to be able to look at a boy like him and think, *What would it be like to kiss him?* and the next second *be* kissing him without one word of conversation in a cool crawlspace stinking of beer behind a crowded bar? We were panting and fumbling with each other's belts and flies; he reached down to free himself and then his hands were back on my shoulders, pushing me down, and I thought, *OK, this isn't cool, the bar back's gonna come through that door any second now*—and then I was hungrily sucking a fat, pale, circumcised cock with a huge red mushroom head, gripping his bucking ass with one hand and jacking myself off with the other. From the look on his face and the way he steered me with his big hands, to the taste and thrust of his beautiful cock, he emanated a ravishing forthrightness, neither scornful nor sentimental: *you wanted it, here it is*. He came copiously in my mouth, which caused me to squirt; the door banged open and a shirtless bar back yelled at us to get the hell out, and I was alone again in the crowd, dazed and wiping my mouth, making my way back out into the throngs on the street to look for Nate.

Closer to home—home now being Casa Feliz, a seedy, art deco apartment building at Geary and Leavenworth, above the Hob Nob Lounge—coming in from the bars a few weeks ago I stepped into the ancient *Midnight Lace* elevator here and found I was sharing it with the very tall, skinny, acne-scarred guy who lives on the top floor. We've passed each other and nodded before; he shows a big box, but also looks like kind of a dope. He leered at me and one thing led to another; we rode the elevator up to the roof and fucked each other on the gravel. He's my guilty secret; he's definitely low-IQ; the little conversation we've had makes me cringe. It's all very E. M. Forster and the streetcar conductor. Thing is, he reminds me of my eighth grade fuck buddy Mick, right down to the awful guilt I feel after I give in and do it with him again. He's crude and enthusiastic in bed, a true reciprocal—seems equally to enjoy fucking and getting fucked.

I was sneaking up for it while my older brother and his wife were here from Texas. We did it on the roof again the night of the White Night Riots and I was dripping nastily several days later, which occasioned a visit to the Fourth Street Clinic, where I found a long line of men outside waiting for opening time. Later, in the packed waiting room, an old bar acquaintance turned around and knelt in his plastic chair to yell, "Hey, baby! Did you riot?"

Steve was up from Monterey with several friends from the restaurant on Wednesday; all is forgiven. He brought pockets full of speed and we took some and went dancing at the I-Beam.

August 13, 1979

Just home from seeing *The Homecoming* and *Butley* with Gina at the Strand. Before the movies we had a drink several doors down at the antediluvian Starlight Lounge. It's musty and dark, with a circular bar supporting half a dozen elderly alcoholics perched on stools, masses of pink balloons following the path of the counter overhead. A mumbling woman in a tiara fell off her seat and had to be hoisted back. The bartender announced on a crackling microphone, "After an extension of fifteen minutes, Attitudes Hour is seriously ending!"

Typical circus at the Strand: constant foot traffic stumbling on the steps in the balcony, suspiciously creaking seats, and the occasional mouse darting across the aisle. No repeat, unfortunately, of last year's experience when I went to *Pink Flamingos* with John, straight guy my age at the store who's become a pretty good friend, and gave a hand-job to this nice-looking guy without John ever noticing. A short, well built, dark-haired man sat down beside me with his coat in his lap and smiled when I glanced over. Soon he was pressing his leg against mine, taking my hand in his, then, to my surprise—I'd really thought he was just shyly flirting—taking out a big, smooth, hard cock and wrapping my fingers around it. He looked straight ahead while I wanked him quietly, stiffening his legs and gripping the armrests when he ejaculated over my hand and into his coat. He got up and left immediately. John was laughing merrily at the movie all the while, but I'd assumed he must know what was going on and would be pissed off with me. Out on the street I said, "I'm sorry about what happened back there; I didn't really stop to think."

"Kevin, I don't care if you want to hold hands with a stranger at the movies," he said.

August 26, 1979
Friday night, after spending the evening guzzling coffee and finishing Laurie Colwin's *Shine On, Bright and Dangerous Object*, I badly needed to get the literary sugar out of my system, and so was easily talked into going to the Stud with Nate and his boyfriend Kenny. Last call came when I was standing at the ice-filled trough peeing in front of the black-lit mirror. A man somewhat taller and fleshier than me was suddenly staring straight at me from a few feet away, and I stared back. He had a kind of wet, sentimental look around the eyes; dressed clone-butch; dark-blond short hair and mustache; Michael Yorkish. As I shouldered my way over to him a smirky voice over the PA system was exhorting us to leave, the bar was now closed; *all you cute ones to the front.*

His name was Cary. We took a cab to his place, which turned out to be only a block away from the Sixteenth Street flat I'm now sharing with Nate and Eddie from work. Inside, I was left in a carpeted hall with a cat named Claire while he disappeared into the bathroom for what seemed a very long time. The place was rife with kitsch and Hollywood: between the frilly-curtained windows (layers of drapery dragging the floor) every inch of wall was plastered with framed movie stills— young Judy; wizened, grimacing Judy; "Judy Live!" Cary finally emerged and we began to kiss sloppily, rolling off the couch and onto the carpet. I said, "Want to take off our clothes?"

He led me into another Smithsonian storeroom, narrow paths running between display tables and piles of photography books. The bed was draped with a filmy insect curtain like a sultan's tent, a pith helmet hung artfully from one of the posts. This atmosphere of Tara or *Sunset Boulevard* was a mindfuck, because Cary, if somewhat paunchy unclothed, possessed a fine fat cock in good working order. He refused to be fucked, though he sucked my dick, drooling lots, then greased up his dick with something from a tub beside the bed and shoved it painfully up my butt. His dick was too big, and he was the kind of guy who likes to pull it all the way out, wait a beat, then jam it back in—over and over. I relaxed into it for a while, but after getting brutally plowed for what must have been an hour, I started to feel really sore. He kept pulling my hands away from my dick, so I couldn't jack off. Finally, I detached myself from him, slid out of bed, and started pulling on my clothes.

"Hey," he said, smiling weakly. "Was I too rough? You're really nice. C'mere…" He bent down to hug me. "Just stay and cuddle, OK?" I reluctantly climbed back into the gossamer tent, socks still on, and lay with my back to him. It wasn't a minute before Moby Dick was being jammed back in me: "I'll come fast, I swear!" I jumped up and yanked on my pants and T-shirt.

"I'm going. I've got to go now."

"Oh, OK, you just do that. Go ahead." He was turning nasty now. It was imperative I find my coat and the door. He got up to lean out into the hall and shout after me: "Why don't you do yourself a favor, huh? Just don't go back to the Stud. It isn't your style!"

November 14, 1979
Gina, my Marina poetry workshop buddy, met me for lunch today. We hugged and walked down Kearney to Sacramento and up to Hang Ah for cheap Chinese. She's been on my mind. She was at Gloria's party on Sunday, which Nate and I attended coming down from acid we'd taken for a hike to Buena Vista Park earlier, and we talked a lot then. She smiles, strokes my arm, leans into me, seems aware that I'm attracted to her, though my official stance is that it'd be a terrible idea to have sex with her, when I'm basically attracted to men. Wouldn't she end up hating me? But I need a friend, Nate leaving any

minute to go back to Michigan, Steve back in Monterey, Michael disappearing and reappearing like a comet.

November 17, 1979

I was resigned to being lonely and depressed last night; Nate had left in the morning, hitchhiking back to Michigan. Eddie announced that John's wife Arianna and several other folk music enthusiasts would be over rehearsing with him in the kitchen later (they plan to record a cassette before Eddie's return to Florida) and I wasn't looking forward to another Young Life meeting. (I fleetingly considered removing all the spoons from the silverware drawer, as somebody's bound to snatch up a pair and play them.)

Walking back from a drink at Sutter's Mill on my break, I saw the back of Quentin Crisp's unmistakable head in the window of the record store next to Bonanza; he was there promoting a record he's made. I was too shy to go in, but the friendly dyke who works there came over and insisted I come meet him. Buzzed on a beer and hung over from Nate's going-away celebration the night before, I was duly presented to Quentin. He seemed quite kind and alert in his, what? seventies?—blue-rinsed, teased, and coifed hair, slightly jaundiced-looking—or was he under an amber spot? He signed a copy of his unreadable fantasy volume, *Chog*, a copy of which I'd carried over, and listened with his head cocked to the side like a sparrow while I told him how my father, Max, had yanked the plug out of the wall when school chum Thomas and I were watching *The Naked Civil Servant* on TV in the living room back in El Paso. He drew himself up and declaimed grandly, "Tell him to *remain calm*!" It seemed like one of a set of revolving responses he had at the ready; I heard him saying much the same thing to a plump woman who'd been waiting in line behind me as I went out the door.

As I stepped from the shower that evening, old fuck buddy Jim Crockett called up and saved me from the impending hootenanny. We've called or bumped into each other at the Stud from time to time since first tricking two years ago. He's a handsome, long-blond-haired hippie, terribly affectionate, and always an enthusiastic surprise in bed.

After drinking at a Mission Street bar called the Outer Limits and then moving on to the Stud, we came back here around one. We'd both warned of being tired and high and probably just wanting to cuddle, but once our clothes were off we began kissing slowly and intently and got very aroused. Jim, who's a sort of cum-cheerleader—he coaxes and goads it out of me in the most urgent, smutty tones—was chanting *yeah yeah c'mon c'mon, shoot it, yeah*, straddling my chest while I tongued his balls and asshole, till I yelled and sprayed my load against his back and he came in my face and mouth. The pocket doors dividing my room from straight Eddie's swayed and rattled and I figured this would give him another fond San Francisco memory to take back with him to Florida.

December 1, 1979

Went to two Garbo movies at the Richelieu with Gina last Sunday afternoon, smoking a joint on the walk there in the pouring rain. (In one, Garbo says, "I'm just a nice young woman— not too young, and not too nice." Later, a giddy matron sighs, "If this is life, I'll take castor oil.") After, we walked to Kimo's for a drink in the glassed-in second story and fell into our usual stance: me chattering and acting like a secretary being chased around the desk by a lecherous boss, Gina smiling dreamily, deepset eyes glistening; touching my hand, rubbing my leg with hers. We discussed it: her attraction is flattering, and I'm also attracted to her, but what's the point of doing it and risking our friendship, if I'm gay? She laughingly allowed as that was fine, but would it be permissible for her to fantasize about me?

Moments after I'd walked in the door back at Sixteenth Street, Gloria's friend Craig phoned up and asked me over to eat dinner. (Gloria's the former North Beach exotic dancer who's now the hardcover buyer at the store. She's been talking for months about setting me up with her pal, whom I spoke to briefly the day of the party at her house, when I'd been too spaced-out from the acid I'd taken earlier that day to talk long. He's about her age: early thirties.)

I went over to his Albion Street flat and we talked and drank beer while he cooked dinner. Later, we lay on the bed in his room watching *Love for Lydia* on PBS, the Twin Peaks tower lights blinking on the horizon out the tall bay windows. A copy of a mass market self-help book, *Don't Say Yes When You Want to Say No*, lay open on the nightstand, yet he didn't *seem* to be an idiot. At some point he stretched, yawned, put his arm around me and began massaging my neck. Then we were kissing with great interest and shucking our clothes. He's got blondish hair and spectacles, a slender, pale body with a long skinny cock to match. He fucked me on my back with my legs pushed to my shoulders till we both came; then I fucked him till he came again and I pulled out and beat off fast, licking up his cum. He gets up early for work, so was quickly asleep; I showered, got back into bed and lay on my side with his arms around me and one leg thrown over mine, staring out at the blinking lights in the rain and thinking, thinking.

In the morning, when I was headed for work after a quick breakfast on Castro Street, as the crowded Taravel streetcar pulled away, a young woman seated about six inches from my crotch and wearing the ubiquitous Dianne Feinstein bow, said loudly to her friend, "Now leaving Fairyland!"

That afternoon I took my five o'clock break around the corner at Sutter's Mill; stood leaning on a wall at the bottom of the stairs eating peanuts and drinking a beer, feeling fortified by

Craig's desire. A cute boy walked over and reached into the peanut barrel, glancing at me. I stared boldly back at him; he looked flustered and moved on, but a minute later he'd thought better of it and came back, standing right beside me. He was on the short side, stocky; big thighs, bulgy crotch, and compact, round ass; wearing stiff new Levis and a green-and-blue-checked shirt; light brown hair parted on the side and swooped across his forehead like a schoolboy's; big doe-like brown eyes. "Work around here?" I asked. He was immediately very friendly, explained that he attends San Jose State but drives into the city once a week to see his therapist. I had to get back to work; he mentioned that he'd probably head for Moby Dick later. As we said our names and I went to walk away, he laid his hand flat on my chest a moment as if sounding my heart.

December 3, 1979
Last Tuesday was the anniversary of the Moscone-Milk murders. I felt very solitary sitting in this room alone aware that hundreds of other gay men were massing for a candle-light march a few blocks away. I couldn't see myself walking out alone to join in, and I felt a pang at having no close gay friend to do this sort of thing with. Finished *The Duke of Deception* instead.

Wednesday night I called Craig, rather than waiting a few more days to feign a more casual attitude, and he was nice, but said, uncomfortably, "Yes, well, I have something I need to say to you...." I knew before he said it: a friend he'd been with a month ago thought he might have anal gonorrhea, so Craig might have it, though he's evidenced no drip.

I bore up and, as soon as I counted my drawer at work the next morning, trotted straight to the Fourth Street clinic. Long wait before seeing a middle-aged doctor who stabbed at my asshole several times with a giant Q-tip before it actually went in. ("Open your mouth, breathe in, and relax!") Lots of blood drawn. No calls yet, so hopefully I've a clean slate.

December 16, 1979

Major leap through time: I'm exactly where I hoped to be over the last few months, first morning in my new Polk Street apartment, all my stuff moved in and put away, laundry going in the laundry room off the lobby downstairs so I'll have clean jeans to go meet Ben in tomorrow.

Ben: Last Monday, December 10, I went to Sutter's Mill on break and sat down at a table with my legs stretched out, drinking a beer. Two weeks before, I'd been cruised by this cute young guy; we'd exchanged names and I'd gotten smashed that night on Castro because he'd said he might be there—but we missed each other. He'd said he comes to the city every Monday; I activated some slight self-control and didn't race back to Sutter's the following Monday, so as not to be haunting the place for him. (He says he was there looking for me.)

So last Monday, just as I was about to give up hope and leave, there he was. I felt a sort of pure joy when I saw him again and he approached me, smiling broadly. He said he was aiming to do something really different this evening, maybe go to the baths (*Or get laid, maybe?* I thought). I asked if he'd like to meet me at Bonanza in fifteen minutes and go to dinner at Hong Kong Café, then check out punk night at the Stud.

A little later I was closing out my drawer and saw him browsing the gay section, smiling a conspirator's smile, and I felt all true-romance-comics, "couldn't take my eyes off him," etc. He drove us to my old place on Sixteenth Street in a tidy little Toyota and I changed my shirt and led him up to the roof to look at the sunset and smoke a joint. Then we were making out in earnest, kissing hard and rocking against each other, rubbing our hard-ons together through our jeans. When we broke and clambered back downstairs, both flushed and cocks protruding, we brushed past Eddie in the hall. I turned on the radio and we fell to tearing off each other's clothes. He has a delicious body: hunky, pale, and very hairy, thick doorstop cock. I was very turned-on to his ass—dead-white plump cheeks and tuft of dark hair at the crack—and fucked him greedily, twice, with intense flashes of tenderness and lust. My cock felt so good inside him: holding his hairy legs back over his shoulders, I could push in slowly and pull almost all the way out again and feel his tight hole grabbing at my cockhead. I could just bend down and get the head of his fat, dripping dick in my mouth, staring back into his open eyes while he moaned and yelped. I fucked him slow and long, stopping whenever I was about to come and just panting and staring. I'm hard now thinking of it, and would beat off except I'd like to save it for when I'll see him tomorrow.

He didn't say until much later, after we'd gone to dinner, danced at the Stud, and come back to my bed to fuck again till the early hours, that it was his birthday: he's twenty-two.

Later

Ennui descends. What does one do once one is all unpacked and arranged in one's swell new digs? I'm bouncing off the walls because Gina's busy, I don't have anything good to read, and I won't write one more Christmas card using meeting Ben as a major press release.

When I called Steve yesterday to tell him I was leaving for the new apartment in a few minutes and wouldn't have a phone for a while, he had the interesting news flash that his new lover Randy's father had stepped into the backyard and blown his head off while his mom was frying eggs for breakfast; no hints, no note. "If you knew Randy's mother and sister you wouldn't need a note to figure it out," Steve said.

I walked out to make some phone calls awhile ago and while

I was talking to Gloria an older man came and stood in front of the phone booth. I held up a finger to say "just a minute" and he signaled "no hurry." When I stepped out he was just standing there: "It wasn't the phone I wanted." This is Polk Street, and anyone of youthful mien loitering may be taken for a hustler.

Coming out of the 'N Touch after a drink, I walked by a record store window with a display for a new Jethro Tull album and some crazed-looking but at the same time very hot speed freak eyed me and yelled, "Yeah, that's right, why don't you go home and think about Ian Anderson in your wet dream!" Instead I went home and thought about *him* and jerked off.

December 19, 1979
Frightening happiness of requited love. Another Monday with Ben. We met at Sutter's, mooned and stuttered about how glad we were to see each other, sat close in a booth, kissed discretely and got hard-ons. I couldn't stop smiling; my face hurt from it. I felt delirious. Soon we were walking into my apartment, really alone (no Eddie blowing his nose or strumming folk tunes on his guitar behind the pocket doors) for the first time. I yanked his jeans down and sucked his short fat plunger, turned him over on his stomach and shoved my cock up him with a little spit for lube.

1980

January 6, 1980

Thursday night acid marathon with Gina: We swallowed our tabs with tuna sandwiches and cut up fruit, then lounged around with pillows on the rug listening to records and talking, occasionally sneaking to the bathroom to check ourselves out in the mirror. Usual progession from "I'm not sure, I think I might be feeling something," to "Whoa, the carpet's rippling!" When we were both decidedly high we wrapped up well and headed out onto Polk Street, walking down to Sacramento to hike up to Lafayette Park in the cold mist. Polk crazies abounded; some guy walking toward us suddenly twitched away and bounced off a street sign. We walked on casually a block before saying out of the sides of our mouths, "Did that just happen, or are we that high?" We had some trouble making up our minds when to step in front of cars at intersections: let's just say green and red have never been so open to interpretation. I'm surprised one doesn't read in the paper more often of people on LSD being run over by traffic.

We strolled in darkness up and through Lafayette Park; climbing the hill, which made our pulses race, seemed to make us hallucinate more. Passing through the dense top of the park, we both remarked on the oddness of seeing tiny orange fireflies moving among the underbrush; pausing to stare a moment, we were stared back at by two sultry men whose faces took shape at the end of their lit cigarettes. Later, we stood at the top of Alta Plaza Park looking at the glowing city, downtown blinking in one direction, Twin Peaks the other. We were touching in an affectionate way, but I knew Gina was feeling amorous and the acid brought out all my complicated feelings about sex between us. As we rushed back through the icy dark of Lafayette she said, stroking my arm, "This is the kind of high you want to experiment with, do things you wouldn't normally do." "If you want to experiment that way," I said wryly, "I'm sure you'll find some willing researchers in these very bushes. Or you can stick with me for witty conversation."

We straightened up sufficiently to go upstairs at Kimo's for a drink. I gulped beers to dull the hyper-consciousness of the drug, while Gina toyed with an Irish coffee. Our pupils were hugely dilated, though surely our condition can't have been as obvious as it felt. Now and then a guy in a very drunk group of men at another table let go with these out-of-nowhere animal whoops, which would make Gina and me forget what we'd been saying, faces frozen.

We went back to the apartment, spread out grapes, oranges and apples on the carpet, and switched on the TV to

find *Silk Stockings* just beginning, which kept us mesmerized
for several hours.

By 4:30 I was ready to bow out; Gina, who'd not been
drinking herself down, decided to head home and stay up.
Would she be crazy to walk the eight blocks up Bush to
Monroe at this hour? There was no way I could walk her.
Later, she said she'd seen herself in the giant lobby mirror
on her way out and felt sure her looks were more likely to
frighten than entice. I lay vibrating in bed. Sirens wailed about
five minutes after she walked out, so I imagined her murdered
six different ways till the phone rang and she was home and
fine, Cat-Bear purring like a Mixmaster into the phone.

I slept till noon the next day. Ben arrived directly from his
therapist appointment and we barely paused to remove his
coat before hitting the floor. I fucked him greedily in the
mouth and came down his throat. Then I pulled out his hard
cock and sucked him till he came—which took so long, I
began to have thoughts even I recognized as mean about the
extent of my attraction to him.

Later
Ran down to the tiny laundry room to check my clothes, and
walked in on three worn-looking hippies, two men and a
woman who looked like they hadn't brushed their teeth since
the summer of love, one of whom had been saying, "They've

taken over the city, that's all there is to it... blah blah... Castro... Polk...." before falling silent while I pulled my clothes from the dryer. I went back upstairs, showered, put on new painter pants, T-shirt, and jean jacket and strode out under a gray sky to the top of Lafayette Park, eating an apple and surveying the conquered land.

I'm not in love with Ben, and it pisses me off. I feel like an ass for letting things move so fast before realizing the obvious disparities in our interests and experiences. Someone who doesn't find out about sex till his twenty-first year, in the Bay Area, at this point in time, has to be backward. He doesn't read, unless you count the uncreased copy of *Loving Someone Gay* I've cringed to see him carrying around. His unformed personality has spoiled all my lust for his yummy body. All this is making me feel guilty and a cad, and wishing I weren't with him when I am. OK, it's also true that, much as I like to fuck him, I don't like being cast solely as top, physically *and* emotionally.

January 19, 1980
Today is my twenty-fourth birthday. I wrote a poem about a rotting mouse I discovered behind my bookcase.

February 27, 1980
A week ago Friday I went to a big party in the Haight thrown by co-workers of Michael's. There were throngs of Jesus

freaks witnessing in front of Kimo's while we waited for a bus, so we were kept busy insulting them as they periodically interrupted our conversation with a non sequitur Bible quote. Then there was a commotion and to my delight I looked around to see B. W. ("Hairy James"), the gorilla trumpeter from the wharf I tricked with two years ago, yelling at a couple of crew-cut, zitty blondes to get the hell out of his face. (He'd been so adorable and so nasty in bed. He took a bath and left my tub carpeted with his copious, wiry black body hair. I wouldn't believe him when he said his job was playing the trumpet in a gorilla suit—till I passed a trumpet-playing gorilla at the wharf one day months later and he said, "Hello, handsome." He wanted me to fuck him really roughly and I complied, but he declined to see more of me: "You're too nice." I hadn't heard that one before.)

Michael and I started talking to some straight guy with backpacking gear on the bus and ended up smoking a joint with him on the street. He was on his way to the Haight to be a hippie; said "man" a lot, said he bet we got more pussy in a week than he did in a year, about which Michael and I laughed the rest of the night.

Late Tuesday night as I approached my building I looked up and met the gaze of a cute guy in green fatigue pants walking toward me. When I looked after him he'd stopped and turned back to stare. I smiled, and he came back and followed me into the building and up to my apartment. He was very hot: miniature and muscled, with curly black hair, a mustache, a tiny lightning bolt earring; and very single-minded. Without so much as a word we started making out, ended up naked on the bed with him straddling me with his tight little butt, jacking off on my chest while I plunged my cock up inside him. When we'd both come he got up, pulled on his clothes, gave me a long kiss, and slipped out the door.

March 26, 1980

Great Tuesday off yesterday, in spite of wrecked plans for sunbathing (it was cloudy and frigid). I woke slightly hung over, having walked down to punk night at the Stud the night before (where I stood in intensely-pressing crowd listening to noisy new wave music, gulping beers, seeing no one I knew and feeling invisible but content). I dragged myself to the Grubstake for breakfast, then came home and rushed new jeans through the laundry room; shopped for dinner; dashed to the Alhambra for bargain matinee of *Nijinsky*. Emerged spacily from dreamy movie to colder weather and light rain; visited dirty bookstore for lube and a browse through some smutty mags. Came home and cleaned, started dinner, showered, and slid into new jeans and was waiting with damp hair and windows open on the dark, glasses, bottle, corkscrew, joint, and matches on the table, for arrival of previous weekend's hot trick, Roger. We made it through dinner, just, then started necking, stripped, paused to smoke another joint, then slowly started up again, very stoned. He's tall, hairy, stupid, bossy, with a big long hard dick, and he fucked me violently standing against the wall, snorting poppers. He stayed over and I managed a blowjob and wank before he left in the morning.

April 11, 1980
March 27 or so, Brian—met at a work party I went to with Michael Harper—finally called me up and asked me out. We had a shy date: he picked me up in his car and we went to dinner at Hamburger Mary's. We arrived too late for seats at a Folsom warehouse production of a leather *Midsummer Night's Dream* (I'll just have to imagine what that would have entailed), and so instead we came back here and sat beside each other on the bed watching the middle of *Butley* with Alan Bates on TV, till he turned and kissed me. I like his body a lot—short and stocky, with a fat cock. He fucked me that night; later, I took him in my mouth when he came and it made me shoot like crazy. He stayed over, and fucked me again in the morning.

I called the next night to ask him over for dinner the middle of the next week—I wanted to let him know right away that I'd liked it, that I wanted to see more of him. But I later learned, through Michael's work gossip network, that he'd thought my calling so soon was a bit scary, it made him a little nervous. He came over, though, and again it was fine sexually: this time I fucked him—beautiful plump round ass—came in him, and then beat him off till he shot his load. He spent the night again. I called him this week to invite him to a concert, and he agreed only after long deliberation, and glib cajoling on my part. When I bridged the guess-we'll-hang-up-now silence by saying I'd love to do it again anytime he'd like to get together before then, he seemed negatively impressed and sputtered about having to have me over to dinner, but not suggesting a date.

Meanwhile, the night after I'd had Brian over, Gina and I got stoned and went to see *Caligula* at the Lumiere, despite all warnings of its awfulness. And it was awful, like being lost in a *Penthouse* magazine, though not without effect, as when Gina and I came back here I found myself seized with a wave of lust like I'd just held a bottle of poppers to my nose: heart thudding, rampant hard-on. I knew I could do it, I knew she'd be glad, and the next thing I knew we were naked and fucking on the carpet.

April 13, 1980
Feeling down. Haven't heard from Brian. I dropped Rog for Brian, but it feels like Brian is going to drop me. Gina loves me, and I love her, sweet and intelligent and agreeable as she is, but I can't be "in love" with her, as she's a she.

Fan mail from some flounder—a typed mystery letter in my mailbox on Monday turned out to be from Ben: "You broke my heart."

At work yesterday, Gloria mentioned staying in the night before to catch up on her journal; I said I wasn't doing so well with mine. "Oh, mine's saved me from suicide a million times," she said.

Steve, on the phone from Monterey, said ex-wife and pal Marla keeps calling up and saying she's going to kill herself because "life's meaningless." The disdain with which he recounted this revelation caused us both to laugh so hard he dropped the phone.

May 1, 1980
Hard to put my finger down on the record and stop it playing long enough to catch up here, not that anything of great import's happened; more like the record's been stuck. But wait, this is supposed to be where I turn to not feel suicidal. This is where I'm supposed to write the truth about my life, then sit back securely believing I'm living. Right.

Wednesday, April 15, Brian and I went to see Sue Saad and the Next at the Old Waldorf. ("Mark my words, they're the next Pretenders!" Steve had said when he called up to tell me about their debut album.) We kissed as he came through the door, immediately progressed to making out. He opened my fly and wedged my boner out and sucked on it; we staggered into the room and fell back on the bed, where he went on blowing me, pulling away just as I was coming, so that I creamed all over the black vintage bowling shirt I'd been wearing. In the car we talked superficially; I know he's physically very attracted to me, but he seemed after only these couple of dates to have made some critical decision about me, or to have had his fill of me, which is painful to absorb after he went to such lengths to get my number from Michael and find out if I was at all interested in him. "You get tired of constant partying after ten years of it," he said, explaining how he spends all his time working on his master's program and remodeling his flat.

My ears were buzzing and I felt tired and happy after the incredibly loud rock music and torchy Sue Saad, but I had to press Brian to come up when he brought me back home. We ended up doing it on the floor; I sucked his thick, shortish, sweet-tasting pale cock with its fat head like a hard plum, beating myself off, and swallowed his cum. I've got really strong feelings about him, feel scarily emotional during sex. Why? He's handsome, intelligent, works in a psych ward, seems to have his life together. Here's the part I'm ashamed of: he's what the ads call "straight acting." Not closeted, not a jock, though he has a nice mature body. He reminds me of sensitive straight pals back in high school. He's just the kind of person I've always imagined myself being with, and apparently he finds me lacking. We lay a long time saying nothing, then I said, "Will you call me?"

"Look, if you're thinking of any sort of romantic involvement, that's just not going to happen."

I know I've been cruel to others in my turn; I think now I've been repaid.

May 8, 1980

Three weeks since the kiss of death from Brian. No word, not even a second-hand report from Michael.

Last night Gina came over and we made a big salad and watched *The Tempest* on PBS, me swilling cheap white wine from Safeway. Knowing we'd be getting together, I'd fantasized all day at work about sex with her, jerking off in the bathroom over a Grove Victorian Classic about a sailor and a girl in a rowboat with lots of smutty talk about "slippery hitches." We rolled into each other during a pledge break and in about ten seconds both our jeans were hastily shoved down around our ankles and I was passionately kissing her pretty little cunt, pushing her hand down to my hard cock. I crawled up and she aimed the head of my cock in with her hand and I slid up inside and fucked her till I came. And lay in a daze till she started playing with my cock again and it zipped back to an erection and I put it back in her and came again.

May 14, 1980

First thing in the morning at work two days ago I was called to the phone and it was somebody from the clap clinic: I'd been named by an unidentified party as a contact, this party being confirmed as having contracted syphilis.

Horrible day, long waits at the clinic, lots of blood taken, Q-tip shoved up my ass, those awful super-penicillin shots in each cheek. If my blood test comes out positive, more shots, otherwise I'm either cured by the initial shots or I never had it. Who could've gotten syph that I'd been with in the last ninety days who wouldn't call me up directly, rather than just letting the clinic call me? I figured out who I'd been with: Brian, Roger, Gina, and that hot guy I met on the street coming home one night, who can't even have known my name. So I was supposed to call up everyone I'd been with to tell them to get blood tests.

I went home early, got stoned, and sat with my hand on the phone for a long time before dialing Brian's number. "Ohhh, Kevin. Um, hi, how've you been?" he said. "Actually, it's not a social call. It's more of a social disease," I said, and told him. Impossible to say if he was surprised or already knew.

Later I called Gina, not picking up on the hints she dropped that Harold, her ex-lover who lives down the hall, was in the room with her watching TV. Turns out they still fuck (who knew?) so he'd have to get a blood test too. I went to the clinic with her the next day and we got stoned after and went to lunch. I made dinner for her that night, and we ended up on the floor fucking again.

June 8, 1980

Tuesday off last week, since the sun wasn't out much, I went to the Nob Hill to see *The Dirty Picture Show* and *A Night at the Adonis* and got very horny, but stayed glued to my seat (almost literally, because my erection was wetting my thigh despite the unusual precaution I'd taken of wearing underwear). I'd thought I might go directly from these movies to the Liberty Baths, but a stroll to Bonanza for cash and back to Polk Street provided time enough to chicken out and opt for the Cinch instead. There was a fifty cent vodka deal on, and patrons were staggering about, glassy-eyed. A pair of space-cases came and sat at my table and, their voices slurring, wrangled over whether to go home together, lighting and forgetting cigarettes, one of which set my *Sentinel* afire briefly. Then a big, lunky older guy came over and banged his fist on the table (making the glasses leap like in a western) and said his "sissy" had something to say to me—but his companion fled through the swinging louvered doors rather than deliver his mystery message.

July 1, 1980

Entreaty from Belle Reve: I woke to the ringing phone Saturday morning and it turned out to be one of Max's weird sisters in Georgia, someone I've never met. She'd heard that Max had a son living in San Francisco, and that I worked in a bookstore. She's decided she'd like to move here, and she's sending me her resumé to give to my employer. "Now I know you've moved out there to get away from all your kin and I tell you I wouldn't interfere a bit, it'd be by appointment only." I was evasive about giving her my address when she demanded it, and she got a bit snappish: "Well, I don't think it's too much to ask! I've just got to get out of this heat and humidity, and I've always loved the climate there. Now, I'm about 5' 11" and I'm an excellent sales clerk. I can work one day a week, I think."

July 12, 1980

Just back from three-day visit with Steve and Randy, with whom he's been living since last fall, in Monterey. On Wednesday, Steve drove us to the Dunes, a notorious cruising zone near Fort Ord. We climbed over a sandy hill covered with electric-orange ice plant and walked along an empty white beach; the sea was that incredible glittering aquamarine-indigo. Back over the hill, we walked through a shady forested area, soon passing several lone male strollers. A slender man in white gym shorts and sunglasses with a blue backpack said hi and held my gaze a moment. I looked back and he had stopped and was staring after me. "If I go with him for a while, will you wait for me?" I asked Steve. "Oh sure, I'll be at the car," he said, laughing. I walked toward the guy and followed him around a bend, wondering if it could really be this easy. He cut into the trees and then beckoned from a sort of natural shower-stall just off the trail, a roofless wigwam of branches and leaves. (Steve told me later that a deaf guy who regularly sucks people off there had constructed lots of these shelters.) My woodlander was handsome and tanned, with serious blue eyes. It was stifling hot even out of the sun beneath the trees; there was a soothing background roar of insects and the surf just over the hill. We didn't say a word, just stood face to face, smiling, running our hands over each other's chests and crotches. His hard-on was apparent and accessible in the loose terry shorts; I'd had a boner since turning back to see him staring at me. I knelt and sucked his cock a bit, opening my pants and stroking mine. Then we changed positions and he blew me while I looked out at the trees and the other occasional man passing by. He stood, entirely naked now (he'd only been wearing the trunks and the backpack to begin with), pulled something from his pack and greased his ass and my dick, then turned and presented his buttocks, obscenely pale beneath his tan line, bending slightly against a tree trunk. My legs were shaking as I shoved my dick into him and started pumping. I was quickly drenched with sweat, only my shirt unbuttoned and pants half-down; men walking by could see me from the chest up; some stopped to peer over the foliage and watch. A very sexy, shirtless, muscular young guy in green army pants leaned in, grabbed the back of my neck, and kissed me passionately, and I came thrusting into the first guy's slick butt. He stood and began kissing our visitor without batting an eye, while I knelt and blew his swollen red cock till he shot down my throat, moaning in concert with the beefy army guy, who'd pulled out his dick and jacked off.

I staggered back to the car sweaty and trembling. "Jesus, you look like you need a drink!" Steve said as we sped away.

September 28, 1980
Two weekends ago Steve and Randy came up for the weekend; we did acid Friday night, with Michael, and walked to the Stud, where we smoked joints and gulped beers at great speed. I took a taxi home at some late point, barely conscious. I had to work the next day at the bookstore. John had three-year-old Riley for the weekend (he and Arianna split up last year), and in the afternoon he and I went up the narrow steep stairs to the stuffy little mezzanine space where the paper bags are stored and napped together on a broken down box. Came down forty-five minutes later, sweat-damp and still half-dreaming, little blond waif Riley clinging to my leg, both of us rubbing our eyes, and waited on a blond, bearded hunk looking for a pottery book. Very Sam Shepard—pale blue eyes, red

lips, beard bleached out at the edge of his lower lip; incredibly boyish, good-willed smile. Much staring into eyes when I turned from searching the shelves to hand him volumes, long glances back over his shoulder on the way out. He returned at 5:30 to ask me out for a drink, and we walked over to ratty Day's on O'Farrell and sat drinking a pitcher of draft beer on a busted red Victorian couch behind a cluster of oversized backgammon tables. He held my hand, leaned forward to look into my eyes and kiss me several times: "I feel something in you drawing me." But Steve and Randy were waiting at my place, and he also had plans. "I'll call you," he said.

It was dreamlike, and maybe it was a dream. He didn't call and hasn't come back to the store. Mrs. Eidenmueller would be pissed to know I've driven away a customer.

October 13, 1980
Saturday evening as I rushed off the bus and crossed Polk toward home, Mitchell, with whom I'd tricked three weeks before, yelled my name from the other side of the street. We had a date later to see *Elephant Man*; he was on his way home to get ready—but first he ran up here with me to smoke half a joint he had in his pocket. This guy has strong dope; I got real high instantly and we started kissing and grabbing each other's dicks. Then he went off to change, and I showered with Devo on loud.

The movie was good, at least that's my impression: it

wasn't entirely linear and I was so stoned I don't remember all that well. I do remember our walking home with a bottle of white wine. While on the night we met I'd fucked him, then immediately got flipped over and fucked back, this time I got fucked, violently, twice. He's tall, olive-skinned, hairy, with a nice, modest, hard cock, and he fucked like it was a marathon, staring at me grimly and yanking me into different positions. When I came with him pounding me, my legs over his shoulders, it was without touching myself, and my cum shot over my face and hair: hot. We fell asleep watching TV and cuddling; he woke me at six grabbing my cock and poking his hard dick at my ass, and I ended up getting fucked again before he dressed and left to interview prisoners at the jail, something to do with his lawyer job.

Last weekend Steve and Randy came to party on Friday night, then I rode back to Monterey with them Saturday morning. They had to work; I slept and lay by the pool reading *The Sheltering Sky*. When Randy got home he announced that we'd be going to a party at a friend of a friend's in Pebble Beach, some rich twenty-six-year-old gay guy. On the drive over, we'd just finished a joint when Randy was pulled over and ticketed for going 35 mph through the dark, foggy Pebble Beach streets. At the mansion—you really couldn't call it anything else—we were met by Randy's obnoxious chum Katie and the host, Mark, who handed us both Quaaludes and asked what we'd like to drink. There were party balloons everywhere, large rooms full of laughing people, a smiling older woman in a maid's uniform frying tempura by the tray-load in a vast kitchen, and flowing champagne. Randy and I danced to Devo, B-52's, and other unidentifiable music. Katie gave us another half-Quaalude each and a tour of the house, pointing out the different bedrooms Mark sleeps in according to whim. (He seems to live alone, like Pippi at Villa Villa Rica.) Then things grow hazy; Randy and I both remember Katie sitting on some steps sobbing drunkenly because somebody'd thought she was a dyke. (That she wasn't was news to me.)

What happened next remains a mystery. Steve, who'd had to work till eleven, arrived to find Randy passed out naked in one of the upstairs bedrooms, muttering "Fuck me!" when Steve tried to rouse him. I seem to have pulled my I'm-too-high-so-I'd-better-go-home-now routine, only this time I wasn't walking into parking meters on Sixth Street, but staggering through the alien landscape of Pebble Beach. I have half-memories of walking down a deserted road through woods and tumbling down a hill, and an image of myself getting into a car. All I know for sure is I came back to consciousness like the flick of a light switch sitting in a chair in the lobby of a fancy resort at 4:30 A.M., a clerk behind the desk pretending not to look at me. It was all very Lon Chaney, Jr. I stood, picked up a pack of matches to read the name of the place—*The Lodge*—walked to a pay phone across the room, and called Steve, who said, "You're *where*?! *Jeeezus*!" and drove over to pick me up.

When I got undressed to crawl into bed with Randy, who was sleeping in the spare bedroom because Steve was pissed at us both, I realized my cock and butt were still slicked up with some kind of lube. No more Quaaludes for me.

October 26, 1980

There's the promise of getting some sun today; the sky's cloud-less and blue. The phone's provocatively nearby, clock turning its face to me—because I got laid last night and this hot guy, Ray, is supposed to be calling back to "do it some more" after going home to change and run errands. Sex was great; now the "and that was nothing compared to what we *could* do" feeling grows. I've done laundry, washed a pile of dishes, showered; now sit clean and pure awaiting next debauchery, got a boner just think-ing of him coming back and stripping off his clothes again.

Last night: He fucked me, then I fucked him a long time, which was a surprise, that he'd let me. He's this big Italian stud, big chest, big white ass, swirls of wiry black chest hair, scratchy, darkly-shadowed jaw. He was tight and literally hot inside; I came fucking him from behind, his head turned to the side and my tongue down his throat. I woke at seven to find him jacking my hard-on and we started kissing—he's a sexy, hard-mouthed kisser—and then we sucked each other till he came in my mouth and I pulled out of his and shot all over us.

We talked a lot. He was a heroin addict in Vietnam at eighteen, on methadone for five years; came out while still in the army. His grammar's rough, and he's rough, in a very sexy way.

November 6, 1980
Have spent nearly every night with Ray since we met.

Tuesday, my day off, I sunbathed on the roof and read "Handcarved Coffins" in the new Capote book, then bussed downtown for cash. I was waiting to cross the street at the curb in front of the Palace Hotel when a bus pulled up in front of me and a teenage thug spit point blank in my face from an open window, laughing with his pals. I marched into Bonanza complaining; when I left, John ran out after me to yell, "Hey! Have a nice day!"

I headed for 1010 Post to vote against Reagan, who'd probably already won, then picked up stuff for spaghetti and got drunk on red wine while cooking it for Ray and Michael, who'd called up from Piss Alley (phone booth on Bush by the parking garage that always reeks of urine). The three of us went for a Fuck Reagan cocktail at Giraffe, then Ray and I came home and smoked a joint, and he fucked me in the ass, then fell asleep with his head in my lap while I sat up cursing at the crowing Moral Majority Nazis on *Nightline*.

November 16, 1980

Can't complain of nothing to write about: last weekend was a real life nightmare, the water-stained evidence here in my hands. My building, 1242 Polk, burned up at 3:30 A.M. on Saturday, November 8. It was arson; the main stairs, the newspapers say, were set on fire with a flammable substance in several locations.

That Friday night Ray and I went to Victor's for pizza. Tacky Victor's, with its trellis-lined ceiling full of dusty plastic vines and heady aroma of yeast and tomato sauce, had become our romantic spot in the short time we'd been seeing each other. Over our second carafe of red wine the subject of religion came up (the Jesus freaks were strumming guitars and wailing tunelessly half a block away in front of Kimo's), and Ray informed me with a mad glint in his eye (the same one he gets when he talks about how the Kennedys killed Marilyn, another topic to be avoided at all costs) that he believes in Jesus—*and* Mary, which seems extreme. *Uh-oh,* I thought, but said, "That's OK, I believe in *Laverne and Shirley*." The other ironic thing is that when I wasn't busily blaspheming, I was putting quarters in the jukebox and punching the numbers for the new Bowie song, "Ashes to Ashes," over and over.

We picked up a bottle of wine at Sukker's Liquors on the way home, and then, before we'd picked up our glasses, ended up on the floor taking turns fucking each other up the ass, after which we fell into drunken sleep. (Wednesday, when we were escorted back into the building to salvage personal belongings, I saw our wineglasses still standing on the sodden shag, half-filled with white wine, half with sooty water.) I was awakened bolt out of a dream to immediate, heart-in-the-throat terror: the door buzzer was braying continuously; next awareness was of heat through the windows either side of the headboard, flickering orange light in the room, male voices screaming, "Fire!" There was the dangerous sound of breaking glass, and the roar and crackle of big flames. We were both scrambling into our pants and coats; I was shaking too hard to connect my socks with my feet. Ray yelled, "Oh my God, grab something important!" There was a stampeding in the hall and voices shouting, "Get out! Get out now!" My wallet and keys were in my pants; there wasn't time to look for anything else. When we opened my door the hall was full of smoke and noise and I have no clear memory of how we passed from there, down the hall and to the right to the fire escape, which had already been lowered. A woman in a housecoat was on the ledge with a mewing cat in a pet carrier. I remember thinking, *Wow, look at me*, as I put my leg over the sill and tried to land my foot on the ladder and it wasn't easy because my leg was kicking like a Rockette's.

Next thing I remember is seeing firemen smashing the entry gate and front door, and spotting gay boy Dennis from

the fourth floor—we ran and grabbed each other, and then just
stood, Ray, Dennis, and I, watching flames shooting out of
Dennis's windows on the front of the building and repeating,
"I can't believe this is happening."

Now here I am, scarcely a week later, already settled into
this old studio with arched doorways and maroon and black
checkerboard linoleum, original Murphy bed behind a giant
door with a beveled mirror in it, one large window onto a wild
garden one floor down in the large space between the buildings—at 20 Monroe, the dumpy old twenties-era, three-story,
faded pink brick apartment building Gina's managed for several years, perched midway up a steep side street between Bush
and Pine. (Fanatics periodically add *Marilyn* to the street sign.)
Gina called me up at the store with news of a vacancy three
days after the fire. But despite this quick reversal of fortunes,
I'm miserable and confused because Ray, boyfriend of the
tumultuous last three weeks, finally told me the truth—presumably—about himself, and we ended up fighting and breaking up for good last night. His original story—that he'd been
a junky in Vietnam and had been on methadone for years, but
had been "clean" for a long time—isn't so. He'd claimed to
have some kind of federal job as a traveling accountant
between offices here and in Oakland. Actually, he says, he was
a junky again quite recently, lost his job, and was in the VA
hospital from July to October 17. He's been living between

various friends' places, which explains the clothes changes in paper bags he'd show up with.

The night of the fire, he'd been carrying a big briefcase, supposedly full of paperwork, about which he fretted inordinately until I retrieved it on the day I was allowed to go back into what was left of the building. In that bag, he says (why would he make this up?) was a heroin shipment he was taking across the bay. Have to laugh if this is true, remembering how it sat in the office a foot from Mrs. E.'s desk at the store all day. He claims his father's a big Mafia type who hates Ray's guts for being gay. Yet it's through those connections that he gets the drug courier gigs. "He likes to keep an eye on me too—once he mailed me pictures of me and a guy I was dating having sex." I glanced up at my open window about then. Either it's true, which is creepy, or he's crazy. When we argued last night and I told him to leave, he stomped around gathering up his stuff, then turned on me, slammed me against the wall, gripped my neck hard with one hand and yelled, "Thanks for being so *nice*!" When he'd left, banging my door so loudly people came out of their apartments and milled around in the hall for a few minutes discussing the event, I propped the green office chair under the doorknob and gathered up all the sharp silverware and hid it (and still can't find it this morning).

I was very wrapped up in him for what seems much longer than three weeks, and the sex was nonstop and very hot. This is a new situation—I want to be with him physically, he wants me, but I don't dare. Having Ray eased the shock of losing my Polk Street existence so abruptly. Now I'm boyfriend-less and eight long blocks away from my natural habitat. (I've just reminded myself of the silly younger Bennett sisters in *Pride and Prejudice* who wail when the regiment moves to Brighton.) On the brighter side, walking home after getting stoned at Gina's is a breeze (she's at the other end of the hall).

December 8, 1980
Sitting in a sweat after a hot bath, sucking up a beer and talking to John on the phone about my upcoming trip to El Paso for Christmas. I'd called Mom earlier to confirm getting the ticket and besides discussing the Continental Airlines strike and the second Polk arson fire, I mentioned my new haircut (scalped, with five-inch tail in back). Twenty minutes later she was calling back, her voice quavering. "I'm about in tears. I won't be able to sleep for worrying after what you said." "Aw, Ma," I said, "I'm blocks from Polk Street now, nothing's gonna happen here." "No, I'm talking about your hair. Daddy's going to be upset if you've got some gay haircut and everybody's going to be staring."

Ray just called and is on his way over. We've been together every night since a few days after the last entry. He's got a new job at the Red Cross, is seeing a VA therapist and taking lithium.

The make-up sex was incredible, very passionate and rough. My lips are tender, my dick is nicked from his inexpert sucking, and my butt is raw from his rock-hard dick. The Godfather will have to station his goons in the closet if he wants snapshots; I've been closing the blinds.

1981

January 24, 1981

There's a direct continuum between today and that evening
three years ago on New Year's when I paced in my Pine Street
studio waiting for Nick to come by and pick up the few possessions of his that were left at my place—a couple of records,
a dish, a plant; he returned the large new jar of Vaseline I'd
optimistically parked by his bed. What he really wanted was
an opportunity to lecture me one last time in his maddening
est lingo about how I'd screwed up our chance at a relationship. Now I'm waiting for Ray, Ray who punched me several
times in the head—*and one to grow on!*—when we got into a
tipsy argument Saturday night while celebrating my twenty-
fifth birthday. I'll grant him this: he knew as soon as he did it
he'd fucked up bad, and got the hell out.

I was on the phone with Steve just now when the buzzer
sounded. The friends who'd driven him by stayed mercifully
out of sight. I felt my nerves jumping and eyes welling up as I
tripped going down the stairs with the two bags of stuff—felt
some of the love, or whatever it was, for him, once I saw he
was looking chastened and downcast. I said good luck and
patted his shoulder as he took the straps. "You give me a call

sometime," he said, and we both turned away.

This has been a busy year for boyfriends; maybe I should stick to tricks for a while.

March 8, 1981

Steve and Randy came up from Monterey and spent a night and day last week. Monday night we took acid and walked to the Balcony in the rain; I'm vague on the rest of the night. I do recall laughing at two clones with little teddy bears in rattraps sticking out of their back pockets. Next day, mine off, we ran around in the afternoon with Michael's new lover, Gary—we took more acid and went to watch dirty movies in booths in the Tenderloin. Steve and Randy paired off, and Gary and I piled into a booth, fed quarters into a slot, and watched a flickering picture of some hunk pumping his cock in a skinny youth's ass. What with the smut and the proximity, it wasn't long before Gary freed his hard dick (had I seen it before now? Not erect, I don't think) and was taking my hand and wrapping my fingers around his boner, grinning nervously. "I think I'm going to have to shoot my wad, Mr. Kevin," he said, and soon I had mine out and we were jerking each other off in earnest, sweat pouring off us in the dank booth. Had I realized before how attracted I am to him? He's Michael's boyfriend, but they're both vocal about their stormy and totally non-monogamous relationship. The film faded out and we went on jacking each other's cocks, our faces inches apart, almost kissing, but not. "That's it, you're gonna make me shoot," he said, never breaking eye contact, and we both shot our wads on the walls and floor. We fell out of the booth laughing and in disarray; Steve was smoking a cigarette out on the sidewalk and looking at me quizzically.

We continued partying on Castro Street, where Michael met up with us when he got off work at the copy shop. We laughed and drank beer and played pool, and hours later Steve and Randy dropped me off at home, where, when I'd gone up the stairs and shut my door, I threw myself on the green vinyl couch and cried till my nose ran and my head hurt. It had come to me as a total *coup de coeur* in that airless booth: I'm in love with Gary.

April 19, 1981
Report from out of the gap; the way I brag, oh yes, I've always kept journals here: big lie.

Today my under lip's raw from excessive kissing with Joey, handsome waiter friend of Steve's I met last June in Monterey. Steve called up Thursday night and said, "Joey's here, and he's coming to the city Saturday morning. How'd you like to go out with him?" I've always asked after him: "Seen Joey lately?" And Steve taunts me, shaking his head sadly, "It's a shame, he's so shy, he never tricks, and he's always complaining of how horny and lonely he is...." This, about a six-foot-tall, former construction worker Italian stud with impressive biceps and olive skin. So I was like, whoa, it's Christmastime in the city.

I was just getting out of the shower Saturday morning when he arrived, cold and wearing a big dorky ski jacket—it was cold and foggy out. Broad chest, nice ass, big thighs: when I opened the door I was almost struck dumb. He was shy; he just kept looking at me and smiling. Steve had said, "He's bringing coke and mushrooms—" as if they were Green Stamps, and I felt fairly sure the expectation was that we'd be spending the night together, but it seemed too good to be true. We were both shy enough to spend five hours together before kissing.

Very shortly after he came in he'd put lines of coke on a plate and soon my teeth and the roof of my mouth were numb and we were chatting away like old friends. We took a long walk, smoked some Thai-stick I had, and then drove in his car to Land's End. Despite the cold misty drizzle and wind we walked way out the path above the nude beach. You couldn't even see the bridge. The moments when we stepped behind trees and lit bowls of Thai-stick were silent, very high, and sexually charged; he was leaning close into my face to light the pipe.

Back at the apartment we sat on the couch talking and sipping beers; he bent to kiss me and when our lips touched, pow! we were all over each other and clothes were flying. When we lay on the bed pressed together naked I was happy in the extreme. I couldn't speak; I kept thinking the word "joy." *If my life ended at this very moment,* I remember thinking, *I'd die filled with joy.* Well, I was so high, and my heart pounding so violently, I felt as if that were a real possibility. My dick was hard and he was handling it and admiring it and then sucking it slowly and reverently. I pulled his muscular, hairy thighs around my neck and found my way to his big, hard ass. The crack was heavily furred; I pulled his cheeks apart and kissed the clean, pink, pursed hole as tenderly as I'd been kissing his lips. He rolled onto his stomach and I started thrusting my cock between his cheeks: this gentle stud who could bend me into a pretzel was going to let me fuck him! I couldn't get it in with spit; I had to get up and find lube. His body was tensed and hard; I stared at the broad, sweat-slicked shoulders, stroked his big hot buttocks, and pushed straight up and in. He was so tight it almost hurt; as if I were trying to poke my dick through a knothole. He turned to kiss me and I pulled out and squeaked back in slowly till I squirted. We lay stuck together and I stayed inside him. After a dazed, dream-like time passed, his ass started moving under me, flexing on my cock like a gripping fist. We started kissing and to my own amazement I was hard and fucking him again till I came, tingling and covered in goosebumps, my hair soaked.

We napped, got up and showered, snorted a line of coke each and ate some mushrooms, and headed over to Uncle Vito's for pizza and wine. After, we walked down Bush to Polk and over to Giraffe, but we were much too high to keep it together long in a noisy Saturday night bar. The noise of the disco and shouting patrons around us as we timidly sipped our beers was painful; when I began hallucinating little red light explosions like flashbulbs going off around me, I thought it wise to go.

At home again there were some weird moments; we were so much higher than when we left, I was acutely aware of being with a stranger, however congenial. I spent a few minutes trying to adjust the rabbit ears on the TV set before realizing I couldn't tell whether the picture was in or out of focus and my effort was pointless. We started kissing again, and it was different—slower, awkward, as if we were both sticking our tongues in another's mouth for the first time. Stripped again, I was intensely conscious of his otherness, of not really knowing anything about him; the full weight of the "dirty-ness" of our acts came over me in the most exciting way; all my Gay is Good conditioning fell away and I felt the clumsy, nasty, forbidden nature of taking a hard, dripping cock in my mouth and making of myself a slave, a sucking machine with one goal: to make him shoot his load down my throat. His cock hadn't always been hard earlier; now it was stiff and red and I couldn't get enough of it. He came, thrashing and groan-ing; then I lay on my back with my hands behind my head while he blew me and took my load.

I slept happily against his broad, sweet body, and woke up horny and newly thrilled to find him there looking back at me in the light, bits of sleep-stuff in the corners of his eyes. Pure satisfaction of turning over into his arms and putting my mouth on his, our hard dicks rolling against each other. I crawled down and blew him in the bright, sober light of morning, and came twice, once fucking him, all of it so tender, as if we'd endured some crisis together. It was very nice stepping out of the shower and having him put his arms around me and say how good my hair smelled—to feel, however fleetingly, held dear, desired by someone so beautiful and kind.

We went for a long drive, then stopped in the Castro for breakfast. I had the movie-musical delusion that people were stopping in their tracks to stare at us, and half expected the waiter to burst into song. When Joey dropped me back at 20 Monroe I stood on the street and watched him out of sight, and felt I'd made it all up by the time I hit the stairs.

June 2, 1981
Up on the roof sunbathing on my day off, surveying the two little cottages hidden behind high walls across the street in the process of being pulled down, the two giant trees that contributed to this steep half-block's old-fashioned feel being noisily chain-sawed down. I could hear Gina's hair dryer humming as I padded down the uneven hall to the stairs on my way up here.

A handsome black guy in a suit came by the store yesterday looking for me, a friend of my cousin's at Yale; she'd told him he should come by and say hello. He had one of those newly minted names—Nauren? He's here over the summer working for Project Equal Chance or something like that. Said we should get together for coffee sometime. I'm wary; the last time I got involved with a friend of my cousin's, a couple of years ago, it didn't go well. It was sort of a blind date, but with mushrooms. Patrick was a skinny, balding redhead with a gaytherapy-group vocabulary who annoyed me so thoroughly during sex, I kicked him out. He'd halted me in the middle of our seemingly passionate scrambling—I might have been trying to fuck him, as he seemed in some profound way passive— to intone in this hideous teachery voice, "*I* believe in making love to the *whole* body..."

I was very high on the mushrooms he'd brought and his "save the chi" prissiness put me totally off him. "I don't feel well," I said. "You've got to go." After some disbelief and grumbling, he rounded up his duds and left. I masturbated happily (shamelessly focusing on my penis and ignoring the rest of my body), lay dazed and daydreaming for a while, then got up and stretched and made a tuna sandwich. As I sat cross-legged on the floor chewing, I began to hear a faint, mysterious noise. I listened to it idly for some time; eventually I became convinced that I was hearing my own name. I put down my sandwich and stared at it. "Keeeh-vin!" it faintly cried. This wasn't my first talking sandwich, but you never get used to it. I lay musing over the oddity of this on-going aural hallucination, till I decided to go and sit in the bay window seat and watch the lights in the street two floors down. A frantic figure on the sidewalk jumped up and down and waved his hands. "Keeeh-vin!" It was poor Patrick, who had left his wristwatch behind somewhere in the mangy green shag carpet of that Bush Street apartment. He wasn't going back to his co-op without it.

July 15, 1981

Michael and Gary called up Sunday afternoon to see if I wanted to go to the End-Up and drink thirty-five cent beer. I met them at Market and Powell. As we walked along South of Market, you could smell last week's huge Folsom fire in the distance. The bar was crowded, lots of hot guys. As always, when they're getting along, I enjoy Michael and Gary's company immensely—sitting drinking and guiltily listening to Gary making fun of people, or dancing with Michael. They both took quarter hits of acid, but I steadfastly refused, figuring I'd just get self-conscious and stop enjoying myself so much.

We left at twilight, walking up seedy Sixth Street to Market, and caught a Haight bus to their place; I was invited for quiche. We were quite drunk. When we arrived, Michael went into the kitchen and started banging pots and pans around, while Gary filled the tub for a bubble bath. "Go ahead and have a bath with Gary, if you want to," Michael said. "It's OK." I went into the steamy bathroom and took off my clothes and climbed in with Gary, and we sat facing each other in the long, claw foot tub. We were laughing a lot and Gary was teasing me and then I had a raging hard-on and he got a more serious look on his face and started playing with it beneath the crackling bubble bath foam. We kept almost doing it, then I'd say, hey, Michael might be pissed; then Michael would come in with a dishtowel thrown over his shoulder and sit on the toilet lid and smoke a cigarette and watch us bathing—then go back to his quiche. Gary pulled his legs up and I pointed my cock and it slipped halfway into him dry, and I started to fuck him and he was moaning and the water was sloshing over the sides of the tub. That was when I was most excited and wanted to come, and would have done, but Michael walked in wearing some pajama bottoms and announced we should all take acid and play together. I accepted a quarter hit, then knelt in the tub and sucked his modest, hard red dick, while Gary jerked my cock.

A little later, as I began to come on to the acid, we moved to the large walk-in closet that their pallet and sleeping bags are in, with candles, poppers, Crisco, and the redoubtable "Roy" (the giant, two-headed dildo Michael has named after the little butch straight shipping clerk at the bookstore). We sucked each other in various combinations, then Gary took a lot of the huge dildo, Michael wielding the other end; then Michael backed himself onto it while the opposite end was still in Gary, and I just sat back and stared, amazed. Partly there was that almost tangible acid crackling and popping in the air, but also I felt almost jolted by the intensity of the sexual connection between them. It was as if I were invisible and watching something utterly private; at the same time, both of them looked at me and muttered shameless, smutty words: my watching cranked up their excitement. Of course their ultimate plan was for me to try it. Gary kissed me so roman-tically my eyes welled with tears while Michael slowly pushed and twisted this fucking two-by-four cock in—but even with poppers, I literally couldn't take it more than a tentative inch. Very stoned on the acid by now, I felt a rush of shame that I'd let them down; I wanted to have done the thing.

After a while—the green-glowing numbers on a clock radio alternately yawning to a halt and double-timing with the acid—we got cleaned up again, Michael put the quiche in the oven, and we went out flushed and wet-haired looking for a store open at twelve so we could snag a six-pack to insure we'd get to sleep eventually. We had to walk all the way to Market and Church Street tripping, each stoplight taking long enough to write a novel before *Walk*, spooky thrums and waah-waahs pulsing from every passing car or neon sign. If a giant pterodactyl had swooped down screeching I wouldn't have been surprised. Back at the apartment, starved, we ate warm quiche and gulped malt liquors and several of Gary's pain pills (he strained a finger last week making pizza at Marcello's), watching The *Maltese Falcon* on TV. With typical tactlessness to Michael, Gary said, "I love you, Michael, but Kevin here's the best kisser I've met up with." "Well, I'll admit he's a great cocksucker," Michael said.

They had a brief skirmish over who'd sleep in the middle, and Michael got up and watched TV a little longer, drinking another malt and burping noisily, before he crawled back into bed. Then, ten minutes or two hours later, while I lay silent and vibrating alongside, Gary rolled onto Michael, nudged his legs apart, and fucked him vigorously, only the sound of his cock wetly moving in and out and his pelvis thudding against Michael's ass and the sharp intakes of breath when he came. Then everyone pretended to go to sleep, and then it was stuffy and brighter and eight-thirty and I had to crawl out feeling like an acid zombie, shower, and take a bus to the bookstore and stand in the creaking register box ringing up copies of the latest Danielle Steel for a parade of elderly women in headscarves.

July 27, 1981

Last night I tricked with the cute guy who's been flirting with me for the last two weekends at the End-Up. (He'd walked up

to me that first Sunday and said, "Do you know what a beautiful smile you have?") He left an hour ago, after doing it again
as soon as we woke—he fucks like a rabbit, fast and frequent.
After he came in me, I beat off for a long time while we lay
pressed together kissing, and when I started to shoot, he bent
and took most of my load in his mouth. He's got a tall, slim,
pale body, hairless but for the small, coarse black patch in the
middle of his chest, and the heavy, black pubic bush; beautiful
tiny butt; thick mustache, which reminds me of a wild West
sheriff, or our pale, handsome fire-and-brimstone preacher
back at Mountain View Baptist Church when I was little (I got
a boner at age six watching Brother Bob holding initiates in his
arms, presumably stripped to their underwear beneath the
robe, and dunking them backwards in the baptismal font). He's
very sexual—medium dick that's rock hard and poking up
before he opens his jeans and stays that way till he shoots (like
an Exocete missile, as I overheard an Australian saying of a
remarkable member at the End-Up the other day)—but he's
also very romantic, lots of kissing and corny little endearments.
While he's doing the smuttiest things he's talking like we're
courting with plates of barbecue on our laps at the Wilkes's pic-
nic. I'm secretly, stupidly impressed that he's got two kids back
in Tennessee and complains about his ex-wife in a sleepy,
southern accent. Gary and Michael hated him on sight, of
course. "Don't you know white trash when you see it?"

"Is that better or worse than coming from a carnival family?" I asked Michael, who did, and he snapped his fingers under my nose and stomped off. Later, the music broke down for a while and we were all sitting out back on the deck, Gary and Michael chatting up this grinning, short, shirtless, blond muscle boy with leather bands around his biceps, but turning to make unkind remarks to Sam every time he walked up to talk to me. "Shouldn't you be following some crop?" Gary said.

We danced for long stretches. At some point he backed me against a wall, licked the sweat off my forehead, and kissed me. When I asked if he'd come home with me, he said, "I thought you'd never ask." When we got back to 20 Monroe, we sat a few minutes on the green vinyl couch while he smoked a cigarette, then he leaned back and smiled crookedly at me, stretching his legs out. In the amber light of the old floor lamp his delicate features, golden mustache, and longish light brown hair reminded me of the *Mud Slide Slim*-era James Taylor. There was an odd formality to the way he stopped to fold his jeans over the back of a chair, standing with his boner sticking straight up in front of him. I hadn't been sure just what we'd do in bed; now it was clear that whatever else we did, he was going to poke me.

"I won't even bother to write this down if you're not going to call," he said before he left this morning, holding a pen and piece of paper he'd pulled from his jean jacket.

"Oh, I'll call," I said.

August 30, 1981

Busy seeing Sam or wondering when I'll see him next. I'm living in a heightened state (and not just when I'm taking MDA with him, which is every weekend); the phrase "desperately happy" may best apply. We had one of those little necessary what's-going-on-here discussions last weekend, and decided to agree we're "in like," and not to worry about it again for a long time, but I was lying through my chattering teeth.

Last Friday night when I got over to his place he pulled me into his cramped bedroom and we started making out, with the other three roommates talking and laughing in the distance at the kitchen table. He stopped and pulled something wrapped in a piece of foil from the bottom of his sock drawer. "Pull down your pants." I did as I was told. Kissing me again and stroking my cock, he wet his finger and pushed it up my butt. "Let's go back out and visit awhile." Then, as we sat chatting and drinking beers, and he smoked cigarette after cigarette, I suddenly found myself getting very high. He looked over at me sometime after I'd fallen out of the conversation: "C'mon." Back to the bedroom, where he pulled off my clothes and then stripped off his own while I lay on the bed reeling and throbbing with the MDA he'd put up my ass. He looked stern, deliberate; we kissed a long while, then he pushed me onto my stomach, spread my legs wide apart, and proceeded to fuck me, on and off, for an hour, and I came twice without touching my dick.

September 5, 1981

Back to my perennial starring role as myself without ___; Sam
this time. Not completely dumped yet, but it begins to seem
inevitable. We went out last Friday night, then he shut me out the
rest of the weekend till late Sunday evening, when he called and,
I'm appalled to say, I cried. I'd been to a birthday party for Gary
that afternoon with Gina, where I drank lots of champagne.
When Michael made some remark about Sam having a free playing field at the End-Up with me safely occupied, I burst into tears
and had to be led sniffling back up Bush Street and home by
Gina. She and I smoked a joint and watched the last half of *Bell,
Book and Candle* on TV and I saw in Kim's corny loss of power
when she falls in love a reflection of what's happened to me.

He came over soon after calling. He walked in the door,
his face grimly set, yanked me to my feet, pulled down my
jeans and bent me over the end of the couch, shoved his cock
in and fucked me hard. We slept holding each other, but I
knew this was some kind of coup de grace.

September 7, 1981

Things improved suddenly yesterday morning at 8:15: Sam
called and said, would I come over right then, because he
couldn't wait another minute to kiss me. Full of flaws as this
statement was, it was the sort I've been pining for. I did sit-ups
and push-ups, showered, put on clean jeans and my Our Lady

of Guadalupe T-shirt, and raced over.

When I came up the stairs, his sister, Rita, who's been visiting for a week, was sitting at the kitchen table drying her hair and Sam was doing crafts—he makes these elaborate beaded roach clips (he put his favorite animal tooth in one for me)—and passing a joint. He told Rita he'd be needing his bedroom for a while, and we trooped down the hall and shut the door.

Whatever he's been up to in the past week without me, he was ardent now: with a lit cigarette still hanging from his lips he shucked off his jeans and shirt and stood with that perfect dick hard and touching his stomach. The bed was littered with Rita's changes of costume and an open suitcase. He swept it all to one side while I pulled off my clothes and lay down. First, the talk, which I listened to without comment: "I love you. You know that, don't you? You know how much I love you?" Then, pressing my knees back to my shoulders, he jammed his cock in and pumped me methodically till I shot, and then went on plowing away for another five minutes, sweat pouring down his chin and onto my face. When he'd come and we'd mopped ourselves up, we pulled on our jeans and went back to the kitchen and lit another joint. Rita laughed at Sam as she handed along the joint, because he was still panting.

October 8, 1981
Sam just left. Now I can walk around all day at work thinking

about him. That's what I do, and I'm not complaining. It's exactly what I want, except security, and I wouldn't know how to act with that. He woke up unusually playful and tender, after another entwined sleep. Sex last night was some of the best. I like it better when we do it at my place because there's room for variation. At Sam's, we mainly go into his small bedroom at bedtime and get under the covers and do it. Here, last night, I teased him, "Leave those socks on...." (His Converses were off and when we kissed or he stuck a leg across mine I was very aware of the locker room odor of his sweaty crew socks.) He left them on, and we fucked around on a sleeping bag spread on the rug, to avoid the Murphy bed clanking at every thrust or lunge. When we got to the fucking part it was long and good, the lights on and the mirror behind us. At the last he was just sawing away hard and fast, sweat dripping off the end of his nose, and I was surprised to hear myself saying, "*yeah, fuck me hard,*" and we came together, shaky and sweaty and starting to laugh.

October 16, 1981
Have slept very happily with Sam the last three nights. I took a cab over last evening; he'd gotten the Halloween card I sent (a sexy cartoon devil whose heart-shaped face and mustache looked uncannily like Sam's: *I only have horns for you*) but didn't mention it, though I saw it poking out of a pile of junk

mail and bills on a table. He's been sweet and attentive though, since last Sunday's typical upset at the End-Up, holding me all night, rousing me to turn each time he turns so we stay spooned together, mouthing I love you in my ear during the night and first thing as I wake.

A month ago, on my Saturday off, I shot up for the first time, just MDA. It was scary, and somehow a kind of intensifying of our connection: letting him do it to me, watching him inject himself, lying back in this whirlwind buzz wondering if I was dying or just the highest I'd ever been. I was quickly sweat-soaked down to the arches of my feet, watching the sky out the rattling window by his bed warping in my vision like a sheet blowing in the wind. I was somewhere with him all alone—further, really: I hardly felt there with him for a time, till I came back to myself and found we were clinging to each other, wet and smelly.

Finished reading Reynolds Price's *A Long and Happy Life* yesterday, substituting Sam for Wesley Beavers. Which is not to say that I feel like a pregnant fifteen-year-old girl.

November 6, 1981
Back to the Doomsday Book: no more Sam, and I'm dragging my diary around like Anaïs Ninny.

We were to get together the Friday before Halloween; he showed up three hours late and looked a wreck. He'd scored a lot of MDA for the weekend, hadn't gotten much sleep the night before and had already shot up that morning before leaving for work and again later at work in one of his hiding places at the mall (where he is, not to put too fine a point on it, a janitor). It wasn't long before he pulled a needle out of his sock and put a glass of water and a spoon on the table. There was an ugly place on his arm where he'd messed up doing it at work. He looked terrible, sweat beading his forehead and red circles under his eyes.

"I don't remember when I ate last," he said in a monotone, so we went down the block to Uncle Vito's for pizza, but he only mouthed a piece and said it tasted like cardboard. "It's not really fair of me to keep seeing you when I may decide to go back" (to Tennessee, where his last male lover and his two kids are). Back at the apartment, he was out on the couch before I'd pulled the Murphy bed down.

December 3, 1981
I got an early Christmas card from Ray yesterday; he reiterates I should *take care of myself* and isn't far wrong in assuming I don't. I'm terrible when I've got someone to blame for my unhappiness, it's like a bad behavior charge card. (I'm sure there's a snappy name for this in AA, but I don't intend to find out, thanks.) It's all because of Sam, it's Sam's fault: I walk home tipsy and chant that to the beat of my steps up Bush or

Powell. The truth is I'm on a regular health binge compared to what I was doing while I was with him, but three drinks feels drunk when you're headed home alone.

Week ago Monday, John answered the phone at work, and yelled that it was for me, then ran to the back to add, "I don't want to get you all freaked out for nothing, but I'm pretty sure it's Sam." I was stricken at once with every lovesick symptom: dizzy, adrenaline squirting, heart pounding. I punched in the line in the shipping room and said hello, heard "Why *hello* there honey, this's Sam..." and, holding to three weeks' resolution, I put the phone down without a word.

I got an angry note from him the very next day, poorly spelled. I'd never thought about whether he could write or not. "I hope that you get a good laugh every time you think about hanging up the phone on me," it read. "You have really surprise me. I thought you were a nice person." The card, a low-end Hallmark meant for a child, pictured a chipmunk in a checked kerchief tumbling out of a Thanksgiving cornucopia, a parting shot since I'd told him how I was tormented with the name "chipmunk cheeks" as a pudgy child. "Surprisingly, I don't even want to be friendly with you anymore." Surprisingly? Following several dramatic readings this odd syntax has caught on at the store in a big way. "Surprisingly," someone will say, "there seems to be no toilet paper in the shipping room toilet."

December 6, 1981

Out for a drink with Maya—John's English girlfriend and part-time cashier—the other night after work, I mentioned that besides being depressed over Sam, I was technically still in mourning for Natalie Wood. Tried to explain how, while I didn't literally want to be a girl, I did somehow want to be *her* when I grew up: smart, terribly appealing, a bit tragic.

"Well, there's an opening now, isn't there?" she said.

December 23, 1981

Two weeks ago tonight, last romance—tricked with Pete Peterson (can this possibly be his real name?), a handsome, trim, sandy-haired guy in a business suit I met at Trinity. He'd followed me up to the men's room at one point and walked up behind me in the stall where I was peeing and started kissing me, jerking my cock and putting my hand on the bulge in his loose suit pants. I think he would have done it right there, but people were coming and going and I wasn't going to risk being caught. Back downstairs, he spoke briefly with his two busi-ness-suited companions, then left with me.

There wasn't much talk; he was pulling down my bed while I was still taking off my jacket. There was a long sexy moment when I was naked and kissing him, and he still had on a long-tailed white dress shirt and Jockey shorts and those smutty black nylon socks. He'd grabbed my cock a lot back at the bar but I'd been a bit shyer about his, unsure what I'd find. But his briefs could barely contain the python straining inside them: when I lifted the elastic band a regular rolling pin of a dick, very red, flopped out. After lots of mutual sucking, he pulled me astride him, shoved about half of his monstrosity into me, and fucked me determinedly, stopping whenever he was about to come and just staring with these pale blue eyes—"Don't move!"—and then going to it again so roughly we had to drag the mattress on to the floor to quiet the banging Murphy bed. He gave me a lot of the old, "You're really something, you know that? You are so hot!" We rested a while, then he was hard again and pushing it back into me and I jacked off sitting on it; when I shot in his face he put out his tongue and licked my spunk from his lips and mustache and came, crying out.

December 29, 1981

Sunday, Gary and Michael came over and we smoked dope and walked down to the Grubstake for breakfast; Gary immediately dubbed the waiter, who had a large nose and protruding yellow teeth, Ricky Rat, which made us laugh guiltily. With time to kill before seeing *Taxi Zum Klo* at the Lumiere, we stood amid the usual fray at the Polk Gulch and drank a beer each, staring at Thor, the blond leather man in residence there. Gina met up with us back at my place for dinner, and Gary did a mean impression of Steve's "breathing problems" at the Castro on Christmas (Steve, drunk, had fallen asleep and snored during *Meet Me in St. Louis*). To me, Steve's still the sexy mentor who led an endless parade of tricks up Pine Street to his Spartan studio in my first days here. To Gary, he's a pretentious, middle-aged waiter.

A tacky late Christmas present from Jesus freak Aunt Jody showed up at work yesterday, she who sent me the poison pen letter and a box of stale Poppycock (which seemed a kind of coded message) when I first came out after moving here four years ago. What *will* I do with this useful plastic letter holder with "KEVIN" perkily lettered on it in purple nail polish? "The children are reaching out, climbing new plateaus," she writes. "But I must close; it's 11:00 P.M. and I've miles to go before I sleep." All that laundry to fold, I imagine. Remember when I was twelve and dorky and thought she and Uncle James were hip? Jody and her crafts—*decoupage!* James and his naughty folk song ("You got a booger, a-hanging off your nose..."). Then we woke up one day and they'd been replaced by pious Christian pods.

1982

April 22, 1982

Rearranging books in anticipation of a "new" bookcase from the store basement, I was shuffling my stack of spiral notebook journals from '76-'77 and ended up sprawled on the floor reading for an hour. This life around me now—undreamt-of, though only a year away—seemed to pale and fizzle away as I read. If that's who I no longer am, who am I? (This line of thinking could lead to a Philosophy I course enrollment—a class I dropped three times at Tumbleweed Tech (U. T. El Paso), till I ended up with the groovy, rumored bisexual prof who threw out the classics and assigned *Zen and the Art of Motorcycle Maintenance.*)

The big bookcase heist went off coolly Saturday morning. Looking in the basement for additional glass shelves for my paperback window display recently, I'd uncovered a tall, unfinished bookcase behind a pile of old accounting records. As planned, John arrived at nine and we carried it up in the freight elevator and straight out through the next door lobby. His ridiculous orders regarding running into anyone we knew before turning the corner on Kearny: "Change direction at once and pretend we're taking it *toward* the store!" As we met no one, this Laurel and Hardy maneuver was averted. People did stare, but I attributed this to the cosmetic enhancement of manual labor. Safely in my apartment, John stood inside the coffin-sized case (the shelves were out) and remarked cheerfully that Mrs. E. might easily be interred in it.

April 25, 1982

I just walked home from an Ellis Street apartment building across from the police station, the day cool and clouded over, other sleepovers straggling home here and there with last night's rumpled bar clothes and slept-on hair (dried cum at the corners of lips? I couldn't see that far). Purest tricking is like acid or some drug that takes you outside your existence for eight hours and then sends you back all scattered and immensely grateful to find your life there waiting for you to step back in. This big, blond Canadian computer student had pursued me at Giraffe last night with all the stops out, then this morning you'd have thought he was straight, he was so cool, so "how did *you* get here, anyway?" Maybe he was a closet sadist: there was a half-finished paperback of Kosinski's *Pinball* open beside the couch. We'd kissed and wrestled passionately on that couch seven hours earlier. He was thirty-ish; nice, muscular body; he'd been wearing white hightops and athletic socks, and was inclined to try and pin my arms down, or lock his thighs around my head while I blew him. He had a hard cock but never came ("I almost never come," he'd warned) but he sucked and jacked me off twice.

May 1, 1982

Two days ago, Thursday, Steve came by the store in the early afternoon, in town overnight for some school-related conference to do with his new job at Carmel High. At the moment he was with a bunch of colleagues in meetings at the Palace Hotel across the street. He slipped away later to meet me, and Buddy, my old roommate, who happened to drop by, for drinks at Trinity; then I had to go back to work. Several hours later, Steve called just as I was about to leave work: Buddy had joined him for more drinks in the Garden Court; why didn't I come as well?

I sped over, and walked, for the first time, into the fusty glass-domed court with the faded salmon-colored stuffed chairs and old San Francisco piss elegance. There were unlikely-looking career counselor types everywhere, drunk, red-faced, and laughing loudly. I found Steve and Buddy with only a minimum of squinting (the two good-looking queers stood out in the very straight crowd) and then dashed giddily between backs of chairs and wheelchairs fetching drinks from a friendly black bartender named Odell and gathering sticks of cheese and pretzels. The people at Steve's table were all giggly and silly and getting drunk. A woman named Sue, draped in a lavender shawl that kept slipping off her shoulders, told me I had gorgeous eyebrows, and a skinny nerd in Superfly glasses, Steve's boss, kept shoving a basket of broken potato chips into people's faces saying, "Just because you're talking doesn't mean you can't eat a potato chip!"

We were wedged around a table to which too many chairs had been dragged; I'd swapped seats to get between Steve and Buddy so I could talk to the latter. I'd just realized he was really drunk—he'd been downing straight Scotches and he was making bee-stung lips at me, holding his cigarette way out and up in the air and gesturing with it like he was Gloria Swanson. "These people are boring me to *death*! I'm hungry and I don't want to go with them to eat. Let's get out of here and go for pizza." This was all delivered in loud mock-whispers, so everyone had to pretend they weren't hearing it. I did some quick diplomacy with Steve, who at first insisted I should go eat with his group, but I managed to beg off and we agreed he'd meet me at home later and we'd go out together then. As I got up to leave, Buddy, not meeting my gaze, said quickly, "Oh, you go ahead, I've changed my mind. I'll just finish this drink and go on home!" I wound through the crowded tables and clusters of polyester-clad drunks thinking, *What just happened?*

I went home, made a sandwich and watched an episode of *Love in a Cold Climate*, and fell asleep before nine. Steve buzzed to be let in at midnight. He came through the door moaning melodramatically, "Well, I may not have a job tomorrow, I don't know...." Soon after I'd left the Palace, Buddy had slipped into my empty seat, put his hand on Steve's crotch, and said, "I want to *fuck* you—or whatever!" There was a hideous lull in the conversation before everyone went on talking as though it had been a terrific and daring joke, and Steve tried to keep Buddy under control.

They all climbed in cabs and went to dinner in Chinatown, where Buddy sat next to the forty-five-year-old blond swim coach, Hank, and immediately fell in love. "I see you're wearing Farrah slacks—you know they make those in El Paso!" He chased the man's foot around under the table with his, rubbed his leg, and set about behaving like an escaped Joe Orton character while Steve sat horrified. "Hank, honey, are you married?" he crooned, and "My, Hank, that's an awfully big bite you're taking!" When the miso soup arrived and the sober coach remarked weakly on his inexperience with Asian food, Buddy said, "Oh, c'mon Hank, honey, you know what to do—you just put your lips together and suck!" Steve said he was ready to crawl under the table when Buddy said, cigarette reaching for the ceiling, "Stories? I can tell you stories about Steve!" They all headed for the Stud in cabs, at Buddy's insistence, but Hank bowed out and practically sprinted away toward his hotel.

While reenacting his tale of horror, Steve had stripped to his

Jockey shorts and gotten into bed beside me, smoking a joint. We cuddled in a friendly way, and I prepared to fall back to sleep—but I quickly realized he was sporting a boner, which he rubbed slowly against my ass. After a period of silent bumping and grinding, I pulled off the black trunks I'd worn to bed, and he reached around and clasped my hard cock and began jacking it. Before long, with the unspoken ease of longtime fuck buddies, I helped him stick his cock in me with only the slightest aid of spit. Things got very passionate then: at one point I was astride him facing away, moving up and down on his cock and beating off. Finally he was fucking me standing up on the floor. As we were about to come I pulled away and sucked him off till he shot his load and I shot mine across the floor.

In the morning, talking just after we'd both woken up, I said, "Oh yeah, it's Friday, isn't it? I'll have to go out tonight, I haven't gotten fucked in—six hours!" and he kicked away the sheet and rolled on top of me and fucked me briskly again. "I love you, you know I do," he said as we wiped up and he lit a cigarette.

May 9, 1982

I just noticed, stretching out my arm to write here, that the inside of my wrist is sown with tiny splinters from the encounter with a stranger I had on the roof today—a work Saturday—at the bookstore. I didn't get to take lunch till 2:30. "Isn't the wind too cool up there?" I asked Franz, the ditsy, permed-blond new clerk, who'd taken his sandwich up earlier. I was tired, and tempted to ditch hunk school (as John and I call our springtime tanning and exercise efforts), for the day and just eat at my desk with a book. "No, it felt great, you really should go up!" Franz said.

I grabbed a sandwich and went next door to take the elevator to the Bonanza deck (actually accessed through the old office building next door). *Shit*, I thought as I pushed the door open and started across the roof—there was some guy stripped down to a tiny yellow Speedo lying on his stomach on one of the ancient wooden benches, probably one of the drones from W. H. Freeman (the science publisher in the adjoining building), I ignore up there on weekdays. I hadn't brought my book, so I'd be doomed to some boring conversation. As I clomped up on the noisy deck, he turned over, sat up, and stared at me as though I were some visiting angel. I was happily taken aback: he was cute, graying blond beard and hair, slim, muscular, nice ass and shoulders, big friendly grin, and, I now saw, a cock that was obviously large and outgrowing his suit before I'd pulled my T-shirt off. "Handsome man...," he said, with a hick Texas accent that went straight to my heart and cock.

We chatted for a moment, then I fell to eating my now-leaden sandwich. He went on staring at me and smiling, making no attempt to hide the boner tenting the front of his Speedo. After the last week of frustrated horniness, the summery weather, the lust heavy in the air everywhere lately, shyness couldn't impede me. I put the other half of my sandwich down, turned around on the bench to face him, stared at his hard-on and said, "You want to play, or what?" "Wah, ah'd love to," he said. I walked over as he stood; crouched and pulled his dick out—big, sweaty, with a fat mushroom head—and started sucking it without so much as a thought of the hundreds of glaring windows on the surrounding skyscrapers, or who else might be working on this sunny Saturday.

May 13, 1982

Not to get too excited over this, but Lee, as his name turns out to be, has been by the store to see me every day this week; we kissed and groped in the shipping room on Tuesday. He called last night about getting together this Friday night.

I left work that Tuesday with Franz and walked to U.S. Restaurant, where we got drunk on red wine and ate ravioli and meatballs. Back here we smoked Franz's hash and he waxed maudlin about boyfriend Daryl, who'd called up from his trip to Utah earlier in the day ("I love that man! I do! I just love that man so much!") Daryl's a shy, skinny hippie with terrible teeth and a speech impediment that really makes it impossible to decipher anything he says, like Cousin It, or, as Michael Harper evilly dubbed him after one meeting, Snaggletooth, Snag for short.

May 15, 1982

Spent last night at Lee's—last Saturday's roof-top fuck. No
idea how long it will go on. He's got a boyfriend, whose picture he showed me after asking how did I feel about three-
ways? I'm physically smitten: I don't exactly feel romantic, but
I can't stop thinking about him and when I'll be naked and
tumbling with him again. He's very honey-tongued, with a
homely Texas accent (from what he's alluded to, I gather he
was a high school coach who got ridden out of town on a rail
for fucking with his boys); great slender, hard body, fat hard
cock. And he's really very nasty—gives filthy commands during sex, does things that surprise me (the second time we got
together he bent me over a desk in the deserted W. H. Freeman
offices where he's been working on Saturdays and fucked me
urgently, then spun me around, sucked me off till I shot in his
mouth, then stood up to kiss me and shocked me by filling my
mouth with my own semen).

May 21, 1982

Monday morning I was hung over and late to work. As I
rushed in to count my drawer Franz breezed by rolling his eyes
and tossing his Harpo mop of flaxen curls: "I've *got* to talk to
you!" A little later I was checking the bestseller rack when Lee
popped up beside me smiling, with a biggish dark-haired
guy—his boyfriend. "Kevin, ah want you to meet Ralph," he

said, all smiley and slippery-eyed. Then, putting a finger to his lips in a silly way, he added, "Waall, it happened again!" "Huh?" I said. "You know, up on the roof, Saturday, with your friend Franz?" So he and Franz went looking for each other up there not two hours after he'd driven me home Saturday morning all kissy-face, after we'd spent the night together. And if I weren't such an idiot I'd have figured out why Franz urged me to take my lunch up that first Saturday. I gave Franz a look; he'd sequestered himself over in the train section and was so madly shelving copies of *Narrow Gauge to the Redwoods* and *Dinner in the Diner* they rang out like shots. A little later Lee tapped at the leaded glass door to the office where I'd gone to finish my drawer. "Ah thank yore more upset than yore lettin' awn," he said. "Ah tole you mah speshul feelin's are for Ralph."

Back at my desk trying to sort out a pile of IOU notes and kited checks, I groaned, "Life's grand, isn't it?"

"Oh hush, Sylvia!" John said without glancing up. He's been making snide remarks ever since he saw me rereading *The Bell Jar*.

May 27, 1982
Now that I've been made to understand that Lee's ardor has nothing to do with romance, I cold-bloodedly agreed to come by his place on Sunday morning for a recreational three-way.

Ralph's odd-looking, slightly wall-eyed; the bulgy crotch and thirty keys affixed to his back left pocket were, as I'd imagined, false lights. Lee and I went into the bedroom first ("Jes' relax, honey…"). We were naked and kissing when Ralph came in, pulled off his clothes, and began to blow me. His dick was tiny and didn't get hard. Lee got very excited watching me fucking Ralph's face; when I was close to coming, he climbed behind me and shoved his big dick into me dry and started pumping hard, and I came, shooting copiously down Ralph's throat—he moaned at each jet, pulling on my balls. We all lay still and breathing heavily for a few minutes, my dick still in Ralph's mouth—then, as Lee crawled up and brought his rock-hard cock to my lips, my dick sprang up and Ralph went back to work, relieving me of a second load while Lee jerked off over my face.

When I got home, Michael was calling with an interesting story. He'd tricked with the muscular hunk he met at Café Flore a few days ago, the one who works Sunday evenings at the Eagle, and he turned out to be quite strange. Michael brought him back to the apartment while Gary was at work; the guy kept claiming he wasn't human, and could read Michael's thoughts by putting his hand on his head. When he left, Michael went to the window to watch, but he never saw him leave the building. I told Michael I thought an alien would have better things to do than infiltrate the homosexual community and serve beers in a leather vest at the Eagle.

June 24, 1982

Last Saturday night I met Nate (who finished school and moved back from Michigan a few months ago) and Kenny at the Roxy for *Thundercrack*, which I loved, and which put me in a horny mood. I'd expected they would go out for drinks with me after, but boyfriend Kenny was sulky over something and they went home, and I hiked up Eighteenth to Castro and over to Market and the Detour on my own. It was one of those uncommon nights when I arrive in a bar at just the right time; I was heavily observed. Two guys tried to pick me up right away, but I'd spotted this big, dark-bearded guy smiling at me through the chain-link and made a beeline for him. I was intercepted by a fellow who'd just walked in himself; he grabbed my arm. "I just have to tell you, you're so ravishing!" (I was looking for Gary and Michael and the hidden cameras at this point.) We talked briefly—yelling into each other's ears over the deafening music. He was insistent that I leave with him. I tried Gary's "lost my penis in a car wreck" line—"and I'm an alcoholic!" I said sadly. "That's OK," he yelled. "I'm an alcoholic too, and my penis works fine!" All this time I was trying to keep up eye contact with Great Dark Man, who seemed amused by my predicament. I was gearing up to lunge at the space on the ledge next to him when a slender blond bopped up and sat there, turning to GDM with a smile. I upended my empty beer, and started past him to the bathroom, and he jumped up and followed me. "How's it going?" he said, and it was instantly understood that we were leaving together; we were out on the 1:00 A.M. street and looking for a cab in minutes.

Tony's a French teacher at B.U., ethnically Italian, big, and hairy. With the Boston accent and roughness in bed, he's physically reminiscent of Ray—but such a different person. Back at my place we kissed and grappled, and soon I was surprised but excited to be fucking his big, pale ass. After I'd come in him, I sucked his nice white, blue-veined cock till he came. It was all very romantic and intense, as with Joey last year. He seemed so pleased: looking at me, smiling, and shaking his head. I was pleased too, but well aware he was here on vacation and leaving the day after the parade.

July 6, 1982
Last night, dinner at Gary and Michael's. It'd been a beautiful sunny day, and then a full moon in the evening. We lay stoned on their mattress on the hardwood floor watching a ridiculous TV movie about a good teenage witch vs. a bad one. Gary, in sweatpants, was flaunting his large erection. "Wouldn't you like to help me out with this?" I looked at Michael, who rolled his eyes. "I've had more than enough—help yourself." Gary got up to light another joint, then stood by the window with the full moon looming over his head, and the big silver dome of the church at the foot of Haight glowing like a spaceship. I

went over and knelt with my pants open, and with Michael
looking back and forth from the TV to us, sucked that large,
uncut, very hard cock till, clutching the back of my head and
pumping, he shot a big load in my mouth and I came, looking
up at the eerie and beautiful moon.

August 7, 1982

Out drinking with Buddy on Saturday night at the Polk Gulch,
I perversely blew my chance with a hunky fellow who'd initially been all turned on to me. I'd gone back to the bathroom
to pee. There were two single urinals under a large, strategi-
cally tilted mirror. I'd barely begun to let loose when a cute,
dark-haired, denim-clad cowboy-type appeared beside me,
pulled out a large cock, and released a manly stream. As he
shook off the last drops, he turned to me with a disarming grin
and rumpled the close-cropped hair on the top of my head,
and said, "You look a lot friendlier than the rest of those dev-
ils out there!" When I came out, he walked over and sat down
on the empty stool beside me—Buddy dramatically raising his
eyebrows—and said, smiling, "You've kinda got me hot..." I
looked down and sure enough, a thick boner was clearly
straining against his jeans, me-inspired. I was excited, but
when, as we drunkenly chatted, he said that he was from
Tennessee, I thought of Sam, and Lee, and some devil seized
my tongue and I said, "You know, I've never met a Southern

man who wasn't a liar. From 'Hi, my name's so-and-so,' to 'I love you,' all lies." Joe Buck's face fell; he got up and walked to the other end of the bar and turned his back on me. I had just tossed a perfectly good wiener out in the street to be eaten by wild dogs, and why? To impress Buddy with my world-weariness? That and a quarter will get me a cold walk home from the Stud in the rain the next time Buddy ditches me. He patted my hand and blew smoke in my face and said, "It's for the best, he was too much like Sam. I was already getting concerned about you."

August 14, 1982
I'm sitting in the orange shag-carpeted den, on the orange-flowered couch, orange light coming through the orange café curtains in the breakfast nook with its orange swivel chairs, drinking an orange Nehi. Any minute I may have to flee to my old bedroom and calm myself on the avocado green shag. Fourth day back in El Paso, and I'm ready to take my Texas tan back home to show off, before I regress to thirteen or turn orange.

Buddy and I left at noon on Monday, driving out of the city amidst many giddy remarks like, "There's our last clone for a week!" and "There's our last Club Baths billboard!" I lit a joint before we'd gone a hundred miles, and we tooled down the road with the Pointer Sisters blaring. We made it as far as Needles, stopping at 3:00 A.M. because neither of us could see to drive any longer without hallucinating—exhaustion, plus my poor vision, made my stints at the wheel harrowing.

After that one night in a motel, we drove straight through. Speeding along in afternoon rush hour traffic in Phoenix, blasts of hot air through the open windows, Go-Go's blaring, stoned, a hubcap flew out of nowhere from some passing car and sliced by the windshield leaving us shocked and then laughing hysterically. We zoomed along curving roads through hills in twilight Arizona with lightning striking all around, B-52's *Mesopotamia* cranked up. On the last leg of the trip, from Lordsburg, New Mexico on, we headed down a straight, empty highway with heat lightning flashing on the horizon, a huge burnt-orange moon hung up on a tree in the near distance. When we reached Las Cruces we decided we had to have a beer to celebrate but it was 1:00 A.M. and nothing was open; not a body, not a moving car, no sign of life: spooky. We got back on the freeway and smoked a joint instead. Immediately anticipation turned to anxiety; five years had never passed and I was bad boy arriving home after curfew, trembling ogre Max waiting to wrestle my car keys away.

Approaching vaguely familiar territory on I-10, I glanced out the car window and saw seven or eight Mexican aliens in black jackets flattened against the chain-link median divider whiz by in quick succession. While we were still trying to decide if we'd really seen them, I looked below the raised freeway and saw a tombstone sale lot, aisles of new blank cemetery monuments in the moonlight, waiting for names.

How often I've dreamed of walking up to that squat red brick ranch house and putting my hand on the door; now I was pulling into the driveway at 3:30 A.M. in the weird stifling August night and stumbling to the door and it felt like a dream. Ouida and Max stood there half-asleep in their goofy sleepwear, looking frail and old, twenty years older, not five. Moments later, Buddy and I lay vibrating, sweating, and wide-awake on a big foldout couch made up with sheets that smelled like the past, still rolling and swerving with the car. We giggled for a while and managed to fall asleep before the air-conditioner cycled off again.

August 24, 1982

Sunday night I was dropping off to sleep over my book, TV quietly droning, when Gary called and asked if it would be all right if he came by in about an hour to use my electric typewriter to type up his labor board reply. (He's fighting Marcello's over his final check.)

"Sure, come on over," I said—and leapt up to shut the Murphy bed, wash the dishes, and take a shower. I was calmly reading Bowles's *The Spider's House* on the couch when he arrived. I sat opposite him at the table and we smoked two joints he'd brought along, while he tried to type his important legal form perfectly, and I tried to be quiet. He'd pause, and then we'd get into a big discussion about something or someone. We talked about Michael, whether they'll continue to live together or move apart.

"It's definitely over. He has nothing to offer me." Cold-hearted accounting, but a typical Gary statement.

After a while he stopped his hunt-and-peck typing and said, "Are you aware your capitals print slightly above the line?" I'd forgotten my typewriter's defects, through lack of recent use—the poetry workshop's a prehistoric memory. So he couldn't fill out the form after all. I sat back on the couch hugging my knees and shivering, suddenly conscious of how stoned I'd become. Gary picked up the porn mag page I'd rolled into the typewriter carriage before he arrived, a picture of "Tico" displaying his prominent penis, ripped out of last month's *Thrust*. He casually mentioned that between Tico and his head itching from the dope and the sight of my dick at the edge of my shorts, he was getting an erection. I could see that.

"Sorry about the typewriter," I said.

"If you're really sorry," he grinned, standing up and unzipping his pants, "You could suck my cock for me." I didn't have to think about it. I jumped off the couch, pulled down the blinds, and tore off my T-shirt and shorts. He had his amazingly thick, long dick out, stroking it as he stood beside the floor lamp. I was excited by the harsh light, for once able to really see what I was getting. The bright bulb and the bare checkerboard linoleum lent the mood of a raunchy detective novel. (20 Monroe is after all the Dashiell Hammett building, or one of them.) I sat back on my heels and gawked at his dick like he'd just pulled a ferret out of a bag. His brow wrinkled: "Don't you like it?"

"Yeah, I like it all right," I said. "I've just never seen it like this."

Then we stopped saying anything. He stepped closer and shoved my head down on his cock in that bullying manner he assumes once the preliminaries are out of the way.

September 6, 1982

I ran into Gary and Michael leaving the Castro early Sunday evening. We headed for their place to get some of Gary's new Thai-stick. As we passed Guererro, Michael saw a light on up at his friend Mark's. "You go ahead with Gary and get the pot while I see if Mark's home," Michael told me, rushing off. This undoubtedly meant that he wanted Gary out of the way so he could tell Mark about whoever he'd tricked with the night before.

I had a pretty good idea what would happen next. Gary and I went on to his and Michael's apartment on Haight. We both had to pee badly as we came through the door. He couldn't wait for me to finish, so he pulled his dick out and peed in the sink, half erect as usual. I finished and went in the other room and sat down on the bed, picked up a porn magazine, and flipped the pages, as if I was in a doctor's waiting room. He walked out of the bathroom with his dick sticking straight out in front of him. "I don't think I can get my dick back in my pants like this," he said, my Romeo. "Maybe you'd like to put your lips around it?"

As always, no kissing, almost no eye contact unless I forced it. I unbuttoned my fly and let my hard-on pop out, crouched on the hardwood floor, and started sucking on his uncut dick, which has a plastic reek, like a new shower curtain. He pulled away periodically and beat off while I licked his balls—all in the near dark, only the silenced TV on for light.

"Stand up and pull your pants down around your ankles," he said, and I did so, fast, then squatted again. I had my hands on his firm ass-cheeks while he pumped into my mouth. He yanked away and wanked himself briskly a minute while I jerked off in front of him, looking up at his red dick. He moaned and shot one white jet that hit my shoulder. "False cum!" he said, continuing to stroke with one hand and grabbing the back of my head with the other; then, "OK, OK, here it is!" and he pushed it back in my mouth and came in a bitter flood. I kept sucking and came seconds later, leaning back and ejaculating with an audible crack, panting like I'd run a race. Impossible to explain the awful love I feel for him, indistinguishable from the lust, while all this is occurring. A few seconds of silent breathing, and then he's all practicality. "Hey, we should get moving!"

"You'd better not feel superior about this!" I said as we hurried down the two flights of stairs and out onto the twilit street.

"Oh you bet I do," he said, laughing nastily; then, "No, I won't think of it at all!"—lest I try to make some Prince Charming story out of it.

September 22, 1982
Just had the weird sensation of phantom glasses across the bridge of my nose (and now the annoyance of knocking over the bong on the coffee table when I went to move the lamp over beside the green kitchen table). First break from wearing my new specs all day. The somewhat comforting consensus is that they are cute; I'll believe this when and if I trick wearing them.

Friday night, alone, sober, and horny, I walked into the Polk Gulch Saloon wearing my oldest Levis, red T-shirt, red hooded jersey: clone clothes. It was hopping, the air thick with smoke, sweat, and the cloying, sickly sweet smell of poppers. Right away I saw this one slim, cute-assed guy glancing shyly at me. He looked away every time I looked at him, but he soon came and stood directly in front of where I sat on a sticky ledge. He was backed up against my knees, chain-smoking, snorting at a bottle of butyl nitrate, chugging down his beer. I started to get up to get a beer and he mimed, tipping his head back and pointing to the bar, 'Could he buy me one?' He brought the Bud, smiling and ducking his head, turning his back but leaning into me and reaching behind to grab at my cock, which began to swell. Then I had my chin on his shoulder, one arm around him. He was wearing a bulky sweatshirt and open jean jacket; with all his groping of my crotch, I felt entitled to slip my hand beneath his clothes to caress his chest, maybe twist a nipple, check out chest hair. I had a brief impression of a hard, delineated chest, strangely cleft in the center, before he grabbed my hand and pulled it away. He had an intelligent, though currently fucked-up, face, nice eyes; I didn't like his hair, over his neck and kind of greasy-looking, but it wasn't an insurmountable flaw.

"For a minute there I thought you might be deaf!" I shouted over the gut punching disco thump from the speaker just behind us. He jerked his head around and smiled, then went back to trying to unscrew the cap from his bottle of poppers. He snorted some and tried to undo my fly, which I wasn't having.

I'd walked in at 12:30; last call came startlingly soon. "Do you want to come home with me?" I said into the back of his neck. "My place," he yelled. "Geary and Larkin. Closer." We tumbled out to the street, walking shyly apart from each other. Very shortly he said, "We're there," stepping up to a depressing-looking transient hotel and opening the door. We got to his place, a tiny studio: I noted a desk with a typewriter sitting on it, a small bookcase crammed with beat-up mass market horror novels—all the Stephen Kings, all that devil-baby, pale-children-locked-in-the-attic crap I'm always having to tear the covers off of at work.

He seemed oddly to be avoiding eye contact. I went to pee in the dark bathroom. He opened completely unnecessary cans of Bud for us, lit a cigarette, put on a record (the Tom-Tom Club). *Enough stalling*, I thought, and put my arms around him. We kissed, and I ground my hard-on against him. He fell to his knees, opened my pants, and blew me for a while, glowing cigarette off to the side in one hand. I stepped back and pulled off my clothes; he removed his shoes, socks, and jeans, leaving the sweatshirt on—and started fiddling with the stereo. "C'mere," I said, feeling a bit ridiculous standing there with my cock bobbing in front of me and him in his shirt, lighting another cigarette and turning the dials on the stereo. He stood, and I began to pull the sweatshirt up and off—and in the green stereo panel light caught just a glimpse of shocking ladders of stitches and scars of stitches criss-crossing his chest, a deep hollow up the middle, and a brief feel of slick plastic bulges and gauze, higher up. *Could butyl nitrate so soon after a heart transplant be prudent?* I thought crazily. My hard-on melted like butter on a stovetop; he yanked the shirt back down and dropped to the mattress on the floor, pulling his legs up, and saying in a choked voice, "Put it in my ass! Put your dick in my ass!" Had I really registered his voice till now? It sounded more like "Pud id id be," with the poppers back at his nose. I was now faced with one of those important moral crossroads life occasionally presents in the midst of the most hedonistic abandon. I could grab my clothes and run, which seemed horribly unkind, or I could stay and perform.

I took a deep breath, at this point the same as putting the bottle of poppers to my nose, jerked on my cock, and straddled his face. "You want me to fuck you, you're gonna have to suck it some more first," I said. He sucked noisily on my cock, which got hard again. He sucked so violently, thrashing his head about, I momentarily flashed on all the horror books and thought of the guy in Kosinski who lures men into peep show booths, fellates them, and then bites their cocks off just as they're ejaculating and dashes away. I banished this image, pulled away, climbed down between his raised legs and shoved my dick into his asshole, which proved painfully tight. I pushed his legs further over his head and started to pump, which was what he'd wanted all along. He had his head thrown back, and masturbated a hitherto unseen, very small hard penis. I pulled almost all the way out, feeling his tight ring clutching at the head of my dick, then shoved it back in fast and hard. This went on for maybe fifteen minutes, till, sweat dripping down my face, I came with that incredible strangled burning shot you get fucking a tightly-clenched asshole, and fell panting beside him. He lowered his legs and played dead.

I felt distinctly that he wanted me to get up and leave, couldn't care less if I'd been shocked, repulsed, whatever, since he'd managed it all very anonymously, I now realized: he hadn't so much as told me his name. Had I said mine? I took my time, just to show I didn't believe he was asleep, sipping a beer as I tied my black high tops. He'd somehow deftly pulled off the Hawthornian sweatshirt beneath the sheet that was now drawn up to his chin; it lay wadded on the floor. I bent and kissed the side of his head (his hair still tackily stiff with some kind of spray) and let myself out.

October 7, 1982

I spent Saturday and Sunday at Russian River with John from work and five-year-old Riley, traveling in the clunky old Country Squire station wagon he talked Mrs. Eidenmueller into handing over for bookstore use a while back. ("Now *Kevin*," he'd said in his Mr. Hainey from *Green Acres* voice, "We're gonna have us a company car!") This was Guerneville on the cheap; we parked on a side street and slept both nights in the car. It's been Indian Summer weather and we had a nice if G-rated time sunning on a little private beach, swimming and drinking beer. Riley amused himself digging holes at the edge of the water and watching them fill up, chattering and singing. I enjoy him a lot: he's blond, fey, and cherubic (when I was late to dinner at John and Maya's last month, he'd waited up for me till he fell asleep, saying "Kevin's my friend").

Saturday night we went to Stumptown Annie's for pizza; it's run by Leonard Matlovich, the famous gay Air Force guy from the cover of *Newsweek*. He popped up at our table to put his hands on our shoulders and ask "Where you kids from?"—very *Andy of Mayberry*. That night, back at the Country Squire, Riley asleep in the back, John insisted I should feel free to head off to one of the gay bars half a block away, but since when do I walk into a bar without having had a shower in the last day? Instead, we sat passing a bottle of chablis back and forth and talking till late with the windows fogging up in the cool night air.

In the morning, as we stood groggily beside the car brushing our teeth with water from a plastic jug, two locals outside a nearby auto shop stared and one said, "Look, there's even a little faggot." (One of the things I like about John is that he's a straight guy who knows what it's like to be fag-baited. His first months in town a gang of Latinos threw rocks at him and yelled anti-gay slurs as he was lugging clothes home from the laundromat on 25th Street in the Mission. "What, straight men don't wash their clothes?" he asked me. "I think maybe not as often," I said.) Now scrawny John got all steamed up and walked over with a lug wrench in his hand to ask these hicks, "What was that you said?" and they backed down and denied having said anything. I said when they saw his polyester jeans and electrical-taped glasses with the shoelace holding them to his head they realized their mistake.

When I went out for a drink with Maya yesterday on my break, she asked, in her best tea-cosy accent, smirking, "And how was your weekend in the country with my husband?" (She likes to pretend she thinks John and I are having a passionate affair and is being very sophisticated about it, knowing full well John would sooner die than have me so much as glimpse his penis. "I'm a grower, not a show-er, OK?" he says.) "Well, it was the biggest one I'd ever seen," I told her. "Yes, I had no idea they made rolls of dental floss that large." (John, a tooth care fanatic, flosses on the hour.) And she laughed her high, whinnying laugh from inside a cloud of cigarette smoke.

October 9, 1982

Tuesday Gary called and said he and Michael were going to pick up food and cook dinner at my place while Gina and I did our laundry around the corner. Michael met Gina at work; Gary came by here meanwhile and caught me beating off (I turned on the bathroom faucet, grabbed a toothbrush, and pretended I'd been brushing before opening the door, expecting both of them). He waited here while I dragged my laundry down the block. Michael and Gina arrived, Michael and Gary headed to Cala Foods, and Gina joined me at the laundromat. When I headed back up steep Monroe with an armload of shirts, Gary rushed past me headed for Gina, "to ask her something important," and I found Michael sitting on the front steps with groceries. Gina'd given Michael a $20; Michael was supposed to be bringing Gary $10 he owed him, and he simply took it out of Gina's cash. Gary asked if it was his money and Michael said yes. So Gary was rushing off to quiz Gina and catch Michael in an artless lie. As I hung up shirts, Gary stormed in yelling, "You little lying scumbag, how can you look me right in the eye and lie to me like that after two years?" (*Practice*, I thought.) Michael responded heatedly, "I'm gonna hit him, I'm gonna just sock him one!" I dashed back out to finish my clothes and allow them some couple time.

When I walked back in later, Gary was busy in the kitchen and there was no sign of Michael. We drank wine and talked while cutting vegetables; Gina arrived with dope and we got high, ate, and drank and laughed a lot. Several hours later, when Gina yawned and began to gather up her things to head back down the hall to her apartment, Gary said, "Well, Mr. Kevin, I guess you're about ready for bed, I should be going too."

"Yes I am, and no, you shouldn't," I said. He'd carried on earlier about how unhealthy it was to almost come and have to stop, which had happened to him one of the times I ran back from the laundry and interrupted him jerking off over the same magazine I'd been perusing minutes before.

Gina left smiling, and we promptly had a great jerk and suck session in front of the full-length Murphy bed mirror. You can see the results of his new gym program; he looked broader through the shoulders and chest, his hard little butt rounder. I was very horny and would have come quickly but he kept saying "Don't come yet, don't do it yet!" We stood face to face jerking each other's cocks; then he pushed me down to blow him. We were both glancing at the mirror and back. "Yeah, look at that, I like to see my cock going in and out of your mouth," he said. When he was finally ready to come he yanked out of my mouth and came in my face and down my chest, and I shot at the same moment, and we were left shaking and clinging to each other momentarily till he snapped back to his usual cynical, matter-of-fact self and was gone before I'd put my pants back on.

October 18, 1982

Woke up feeling like hell Saturday, after snorting crystal with Michael at the Stud the night before. Read, lay in the sun on the roof, walked to the Magazine and bought some used porn and came home and beat off a couple times. Still felt awful when the phone rang and it was John reminding me of the Bookseller's Dinner; I had twenty minutes to pull myself together before being picked up. I sat with John and Maya and made fun of the more pompous reps, conspired drunkenly with the cool ones. Two elderly small press scions shared our table and Reynard from the store, caught in a long boring conversation with them, turned to me saying, "Well, ah, Kevin here could probably tell you more about that...," and I kicked him hard under the table and took a large bite of bread. *Chronicle* Book Review editor Pat Holt only spoke for an hour, after which we fled.

I felt better on Sunday. That evening I pulled on clean jeans and my favorite faded green T-shirt and walked down to Polk. Grew depressed over a beer at the Giraffe; hiked down to the Cinch in twilight cool for a draft; then broke resolve and headed back down Polk to the Polk Gulch, where I soon found myself standing alongside a rather handsome husky black guy. He smiled at me, we said hi and exchanged names. Still edgy from the weekend's excesses and now drunk from three or four beers, I said whatever came into my head. "Got any bandages under there?" I said, poking his leather jacket, thinking of my macabre trick there a few weeks ago. I asked what he did for a living, and he smilingly said "None of your business," which seemed unfriendly, so I put down my beer and went to pee and leave.

As soon as I'd got my cock out and started to piss, someone came in and stood at the urinal beside me. I glanced over and it was him, holding an already huge and growing cock and slowly jacking it and smiling slyly at me. Now I knew his vocation. We put our dicks back in our pants and walked straight out of the bar without another word.

His name, he says, is Darius Turner. He lives in some hotel at Turk and Franklin. We walked up Bush to Monroe, mostly silent. Inside, he went into the bathroom a moment, walked back out with his pants open and monster dick jutting out in front of him and we began groping and rubbing our cocks together. He had a burly, hard body; chest, stomach, and pelvis matted with tight curls; fat, pretty cock (several gradations of color from black to pink at the unsheathed, wet head, like a Dreamsicle). I got down and sniffed around (huge balls in a gray-black sack—were there more than two in there?—and then struggled to get some portion of his dick in my mouth.

I pulled out the bed while he got his jackboots and black jeans off. I put a lot of spit on my butt and his cock and backed into him. It hurt so bad I jumped right off, but after several tries he slid it in and I was swept into my pornographic role: White Punk getting plowed by Big Black Dude. The stream of muttered smut-talk from him did nothing to discourage this typecasting ("I'm gonna rape your skinny white ass with my big black dick! Shut up and take it before I pull it out and shove it back down your throat, punk!" I shushed the part of my mind that was already racing ahead to imagine how Steve and I would howl when I repeated all this on the phone the next day). He kept pulling my hands away from my own dick and pinning them down. "Why don't you move all those fucking plants off the table and pull it over to the mirror?" I did as he said, and dragged the high narrow table over in front of the six-foot-high mirror in the Murphy bed door. I climbed up onto the table and knelt with my head down and ass in the air and yelped when, grasping my thighs tightly, he shoved his cock back in in one stroke. Now he reached around and started to jack me off, piston-pumping in and out of my ass, describing the action for me as if I were a Blind White Punk: "Yeah, big black dick going in and out of you. Gonna rape that white ass... Gonna shoot a big load up inside you, boy..." He groaned, ground into me, said, "Shit! I didn't want to do that!"—and came. I pulled off and turned around; his cock was clean and hard, and I sucked on it till I ejaculated at his feet.

October 26, 1982

Gary dropped by the bookstore this afternoon at three to return *Edie* and the Bowles book I'd loaned him. I took my break and went next door to Wendy's for coffee with him while he ate two orders of fries. As we were leaving he made eye contact with this little muscle stud with a military haircut and said good-bye abruptly, which hurt my feelings, though I should know better.

I've claimed to several people to have picked up a disease from my last trick: DSD—Diminished Sexual Desire. I hadn't even wanted to beat off since last Tuesday, up till last evening.

October 29, 1982

Gary called to see if Gina and I would like to make dinner here. I came home, exercised, bathed; had an old Blondie tape cranked up when he arrived. We walked to Cala, and he began to tell me about the hot little Marine he'd picked up in front of Wendy's after coffee with me the other day. I teased him about not believing any of his stories, and he glared at me and snapped, "When I'm with you, I realize just how alone I am," and I said, quite seriously, "Me too, exactly." This was followed by a shocked silence on both our parts. We might as well be a couple: we bickered in the grocery store. He snatched the package of dry spaghetti sauce mix I like to use out of my hand and insisted on reading me all the chemicals on the label as if he were giving me a traffic citation. "I don't want to be dying of cancer like your mother and my father when I'm their age, from eating crap like this!" When I raised the issue of French fries he stormed off to the produce department in disgust.

Back here we smoked a joint, which seemed to have a calming effect, and he set about making the sauce. He grabbed my ass and I squirmed away, ignoring the usual remarks about the current condition of his cock. Gina arrived, toting the irritable Cat-Bear, who disappeared into my closet for the evening and busied herself throwing up on a pile of socks. We ate, drank red wine, and laughed a lot; watched a documentary about gay power on PBS. Gina made signs of leaving, and Gary jumped up to help her carry stuff back down the hall to her apartment. "Bye," I said.

"Oh no, I'm coming back, if that's all right," he said.

I was sitting on the couch looking at the TV when he walked back in. He sat beside me, grabbed and twisted a nipple through my T-shirt and said, "*Would* you like to suck my cock?" I smiled, looking at the floor, and nodded my head.

There was a rush of sheer horniness; all my grievances mean nothing when faced with his eager face and musky, fat cock, and we're momentarily united by the same urgent goal. We hastily pulled off our shirts and yanked our pants down; I started kissing and licking his hard cock in front of the mirror. I pulled down the Murphy bed; we shucked our shoes and pants. He wanted to fuck me standing, bent over the side of the bed. It hurt like hell, my ass too tensed up, and I lurched away. "C'mon, Kevin, c'mon, let me in," he said, and that was all it took; soon he was pushing his long cock all the way up me. I was hard and beating off furiously. He pushed me up onto the bed on my knees, head down and ass in the air, and pounded away. We were in that completely other sex place outside time or personality or petty disagreements. He was saying, "Yeah, you do like that, don't you? I like it too," and nipped at my shoulder, then stopped, said, "Don't move, don't move!" He pulled out, sat back on his haunches with his hand just to the side of his dick but not touching it, as if he were introducing it to me, and I beat off staring as his dick jerked up and started shooting the first of five or six jets and I came just seeing it and fell back on the bed.

"Now, aren't I a good mean and nasty fuck?" he asked, pulling on his jeans. I laughed and rolled around the bed for answer.

November 16, 1982
My apartment is freezing, and has been for a week. Speaking of freezing, last sex with Gary was a week ago, so true to form he's cold shouldering me for a bit. I'd called to invite him out for pizza with Gina and me; he preferred to come over and cook. He met me at Cala, where I'd walked straight from work. John, who'd walked me part of the way, had said, "Is it true that Gary only sees you when he's too tired to beat off?" I dutifully repeat this to Gary later as we're lugging groceries up Pine. "Why do you always have to talk about it?" he says angrily, oddly echoing Mom's old refrain. "And I wish you wouldn't mention me in your little diary!" "What makes you so sure I do?" I said. "And it's a *journal*." "Whatever, I don't like the idea of someone reading about my private business." "Gee, sorry, I think I lost that confidentiality agreement up

your butt," I said, and he stalked a block ahead of me the rest of the way to Monroe.

The usual drill: dope and wine, dinner with Gina, something elevating or funny on TV; Gina stands and stretches, gathers up her pot box and bong and is kissed good-night; Gary lingers. "What kind of jockey shorts did you end up buying?" I asked. (He'd mentioned shopping Macy's men's underwear department earlier in the day—and blowing a nineteen-year-old "straight" boy who'd been trying on bathing trunks in the next stall.) This was risky; if I make the first sign, he's perversely likely to pretend not to know what I'm talking about and leave. I can't seem to be expecting it. But he spread his legs, unbuttoned his fly and hauled his dick out: "Actually, I'm not wearing any underwear." I stripped off my pants, squatted at his feet and unlaced and removed his army boots, while he stroked his hardening cock; then I stood, and staggered between his legs to fuck him in the mouth. I knelt again and tugged his jeans off, and then we both stood, dick to dick, thrusting, my hand around both our cocks. I got down and sucked him, moved under his tightly drawn-up balls, and wolfed between his pale tight cheeks, then stood and pushed my cock in where my mouth had been, and fucked him ("Careful, careful!" he hissed), one hand on the wall, one arm around his waist, and we shot simultaneously, mine up inside him, his splattering the lino.

November 24, 1982

Brisk day at the bookstore. Gary called to see if I wanted to go to dinner at U.S. Restaurant in North Beach. He arrived while I was still in the tub, and stood chatting and passing a joint back and forth till I finished, then handed me my towel. He said he wishes he had someone who'd listen to him talk, then forget everything he said. (And someone who'd fuck with him, then forget about it till the next time, no doubt.) Later, after a pleasant enough evening out, he hinted about staying over, since he'd be coming back early in the morning to put the turkey on for our dinner with Gina, her mother, and Michael (if he should reappear from his current two-week disappearance), but then left "to pick someone up." The companionship he's been lavishing on me lately has felt good, and I make an effort not to expect more of him. I'll miss him when he leaves in a few weeks for a month back in Hooterville, or wherever his father's farm is, and Chicago.

December 29, 1982

One day last week I got a cheesy Christmas card from Ray (kitten batting around a Christmas ornament) and I had a sinking feeling then. Knowing him, it was a kind of time bomb: he would only send me a card with the expectation of getting one back, or else. So I walk in with an armload of laundry yesterday evening and the phone's ringing. A muffled voice says, "Hi," in a nasty tone. Silence, while I figured out who it was: Ray? "Thanks for the Christmas card!" he says.

"I'm sorry, Ray, I just haven't sent any cards this year."

"Well, can we get together for a drink?" He sounded angry and deranged, so that didn't seem very inviting.

"Ray, I just don't want to get involved again."

"I got me a new boyfriend! I'm talking about friendship!"

"Ray, it's been practically two years, we don't even know each other anymore." (I didn't add "and we never did;" virtually everything he had told me about himself had turned out to be fabricated.)

"Fine. Merry Christmas and a happy New Year to you!" he screamed, and hung up. The phone started ringing again immediately and I unplugged it.

He must have been in a phone booth nearby, because it couldn't have been ten minutes before the door buzzer went off, loud and long. I was trapped. The buzzer went back on and stayed on; he wasn't going to let me pretend I'd rushed out. The twenty Mexican nationals in the studio next door buzz strangers in all day long without finding out who's at the door, so it wouldn't be long before he was kicking in my flimsy apartment door and denting the plaster with my head. What could I do? I stomped downstairs to the lobby; he stood outside the big plate glass door, fists clenched, hopping around like a sparring boxer, or Rumpelstiltskin. "What are you doing here? Go away!" I yelled through the door.

"I want my stuff! You got my hammer and my running clothes!" (The last, ill-advised time we'd gotten together, he'd been carrying a crumpled paper grocery bag with some junk in it, which ended up left behind; I'd dropped it in the back of the closet and never thought of it again. If it contained a hammer, this wasn't the time to hand it over.)

"It's been a year and a half, I don't even know what you're talking about. If you think I've got something of yours, make a list and bring it by the store." He was screaming and kicking the door, which, to my surprise, didn't fly open. (While all this was unfolding, a little Asian lady pulling a laundry cart came out of her apartment and started toward the door, saw Ray, and went back into her apartment.)

"You FAGGOT, you're afraid to open this door!" He backed up and did a little running Kung Fu kick at the glass. "FAG-GOT!" I felt as if I'd woken up inside the episode of *Falconcrest* I'd been watching with Gina the night before. Lorenzo Lamas had a habit of flying off the handle like this. What would Jane Wyman do at such a moment? "I'm calling the police, Ray," I yelled, and ran back upstairs. The buzzer was shrieking as I shut my door, and I wondered how many seconds it would take for him to break down the front door, how I would pay for its repair later, assuming my brains were still where they belonged.

I plugged in the phone and called the store; John was still

there. John loves to take charge in an emergency: "Stay where you are, I'll be right over." Meanwhile, the buzzer had reached a crescendo, then made a sort of strangled sound and fell silent. Ten minutes later John was outside my apartment door singing "If I Had a Hammer." "Kevin, it's me, he's gone. You'd better come see this." We went out to the front stoop. On the little brass tenant directory, the white plastic button next to "#8" was gone—some shards lay on the ground—and several wires dangled down.

Some people just can't handle the holidays.

December 31, 1982

Shock of being with Michael again last night, after not seeing or hearing from him for a month. I walked into Polk Gulch Saloon, scanning the crowd to make sure no Ray threatened before putting my glasses in my pocket, and spied Michael seated on a ledge at the back. It was like meeting a ghost; he seemed neither pleased nor displeased to see me. He's fallen back on his old ways, serially tricking; he can't go back to his new place till he pays the rent he owes. He's moving back to Florida in the next month or two. He came home with me to sleep over, and we lay awake talking. "He's the love of my life," he said of Gary. "I think we'll get back together for good eventually."

1983

January 16, 1983

I stopped at Twin Peaks at 11:30 last night meaning to give up on anything happening and just nurse a Bud till a bus came along. I sat on a couch at the back, and very soon a rangy-looking thirty-five-ish guy with floppy ash-blond hair came and sat down beside me. I don't remember how we started talking, but we did, and soon he was discreetly rubbing my leg and I had a hard-on. He asked if I'd like to go home with him, way out in Noe Valley. "Sure," I said.

From the bus stop to his apartment he held my hand in this death grip, which was a bit out of the ordinary, I thought. I was all moony then, and wanted to kiss, but he said, "Just wait." When we stepped into his flat and I put my arms around him and tried to kiss him, he grabbed a fistful of my T-shirt and shoved me roughly against the wall. I wasn't afraid; it didn't seem like genuine violence.

"Whoa, wait a minute," I said. "What's the hell's wrong with you?"

He stepped back, shamefaced. "I just sensed it was what you wanted."

After some necking and grappling with belt buckles and

flies we duck-walked into his room and he sucked my cock for a while. I sucked his, which was of a disappointingly disproportionate size to his lanky frame, but still hard and interested. No, I didn't want to be fucked by him. Well then would I fuck him? That I would do. In the end, I jerked him off as I fucked him astride me on a couch, and bent to take his cum as he shot; pulled out and jacked off till I blew my wad all over him, my legs jerking.

Just as we were ejaculating, there was the sound of a key in the door. "That's my straight roommate, Beth Ann," he said. "She doesn't know I might be gay. Keep your voice down." I wasn't very cooperative, laughing heartily, asking what Beth Ann would make of my shoes, glasses, and T-shirt scattered around the kitchen. He clattered out comically serious to retrieve them, closing the door carefully on the way out and back in. That was when I noticed he had about ten different kinds of saws artfully mounted on the wall. "Collect saws, do you?" I asked.

"I do some carpentry," he said. Glancing at his bookshelf, I noted among his boring law texts (he'd mentioned passing the bar recently) several Samuel Beckett titles, which seemed more ominous than the saws.

"I'm telling you right now, I'm not dropping out of any window!" I said.

"Shhh! Lower your voice!" He'd altered, assumed an

embarrassed expression since we'd pulled our pants up. Then, a mood shift: "Can I blow you again?"

"Naw," I said, with an eye on the tool collection. "I've gotta get back across town, and anyway Beth Ann might hear."

He turned before opening the bedroom door and admonished me to "Keep your head down and just follow me." He walked me to the waiting J-Church trolley, saying it was probably hard for me to understand a fellow living in San Francisco, thirty-five years old, and not having decided for sure if he was gay. "I do go out with women, see?"

I considered the enthusiasm with which his ass was bucking while I was sticking it in him, but said nothing. We shook hands, oddly, just a couple of guys back from bowling, and I ran for the streetcar.

February 4, 1983

A week ago Tuesday, my last weekday off, I went out with a nearly-finished Iris Murdoch, *An Unofficial Rose*, and read at Café Flore; walked around a lot. Later in the afternoon, I bussed back downtown and went for a beer at Sutter's Mill—oops, there was Pete Peterson squirming when he saw me; I took my beer elsewhere. An older, mousey guy, wearing glasses, in a business suit, approached where I sat and asked if he might sit down. "Sure," I said. "What are you reading?" he wanted to know, spying my facedown book. He turned out to be a big Murdoch fan, told me which he thinks are good, which not. Art—he didn't look like an "Art"—sells advertising for the newspaper. After a drink, he asked if I'd come home with him. I, rudely I suppose, thought it over awhile before saying yes—and thought, as we walked to his car, *Am I making a terrible mistake?*

We drove to an apartment on Upper Church, overlooking Dolores Park. I went straight to the bathroom to pee, and felt depressed by all the framed movie star portraits. How old was this guy, anyway? We got undressed and into bed without prelude. Then we were just naked and touching each other in his nice big clean bed, and without his glasses he was a bit better-looking and I wasn't at all too drunk to be hard and horny. He paid lots of attention to my cock: I fucked him in the mouth for a long time (and was well-shredded by his teeth, but never mind). He had a nice plump butt, but wouldn't be fucked, and made no attempt to do so to me. I shot a load down his throat, which he took with great enthusiasm. He hadn't been erect at first, but he was now, and I slid down and sucked his short, very fat, marble-white cock. Now I noticed he actually had a nice build, big arms, furry chest with gray mixed in, red, flat nipples. He seemed surprised by my reciprocating; I jacked him off watching his large balls jump and took his cock back in my mouth as he began to tense and spurt, and I swallowed his copious load.

We napped and talked on and off. There was a huge Victorian lithograph in an elaborate frame on the wall at the foot of the bed: "Mrs. Washington's Reception."

February 8, 1983
Gary called Sunday morning to see if I wanted to go down to the End-Up and dance. It was pouring outside the whole time we were there, making a pretty effect when I stared through the crowded dance floor to the sheet of rain in the wide openings to the deck at either end. When sufficient beers had been consumed between us for such things to be said, we had a brief, scary chat about "why sex stopped." "You couldn't handle it," he says. But what I couldn't handle was it stopping. We took a cab to Bonanza, roaring drunk, to cash a check. Once in the dark, empty store Gary ran straight back to the *Flesh, Meat,* and *Sex* books, teasing me, so recently after the touchy discussion, "Let's go in the back and beat off over these!"

We phoned and found Gina at home, stoned and finishing off a carton of ice cream with Michael, who left before we got there. Gina politely declined to say if he'd borrowed any money when Gary asked. At Vito's Gary and I took turns reading aloud headlines from *Flesh* while waiting for our pizza ("Cop Sniff's Marine's Dirty Jock"), Gina shushing us as our waitress approached.

But Gary wouldn't come home with me, and I woke the

next day depressed and hung over, and called in sick. Barbara, the giddy new cashier (fresh off the potato truck from Minnesota), called to see how I was feeling and chirped about her latest weekend "Lifespring" experience. ("Wifespring," John called it; she and her effeminate husband are clearly headed for new partners.) "You'll laugh, I know, but I just want to say that I love you, and you'd be surprised to know how many other people love you too!" Then I threw up and felt much better.

July 15, 1983

The second half of my vacation materialized with a call from Steve suggesting I take the bus to Monterey. The Wednesday night after I arrived I ended up fucking with Robbie, the very cute nineteen-year-old waiter who works with Steve. It was purely that kind of time-suspended tricking where you put on your clothes the next day and act as though nothing's happened—one minute we were having sex again in the morning, half under a blanket on the living room floor, Steve and Randy stepping around us getting ready for work, and the next, when I came back from brushing my teeth, he was dressed and smoking and talking with Steve at the kitchen table. The night before we'd sat around the same table drinking and talking for hours. Around eleven, Randy left the room without a word and passed out on a couch. Steve sloshed the remaining vodka into our tumblers and said, "Doesn't anyone want to get laid? Let's go to the bar, c'mon," and Robbie ground out a cigarette and turned to me and said, "Would you want to just stay here and have sex with me?" and I nearly fell over backward in my rickety chair.

Steve left for the After Dark, and Robbie and I trooped off to his bed at the other end of the house. We were quite drunk. There was lots of frantic kissing, his small, rubbery mouth tasting of vodka and the watermelon candy he'd been sucking. I recall some complications involving trying to remove my pants without first taking off my shoes. Robbie's coltish and slightly effeminate with his gesturing cigarette and flying wrists—but he actually has a nicely defined chest and biceps; tiny waist and compact little butt—he bikes everywhere. His long body is olive-colored to begin with and darkly tanned as well and hairless but for an inky black bush of wiry pubic hair and a dense, hidden tuft of the same between his tight cheeks. His cock was modest but quite hard and curving straight up his stomach—I had to pry it downward to suck it. Before long he rolled onto his stomach and spread his legs apart, and I slicked my dick up with spit and shoved it into his snug hole. He moaned and bucked under me, jacking himself off: "Go on, fuck me till you come." I lay stretched out on that long, sweet body, both of us slippery with sweat, my arms locked around his chest, and plowed away at him, yanking out to shoot on his perfect ass.

Later, Steve came in and woke us up to reclaim his bed, dying to tell about the "straight" catamaran racer he'd met under the pier who wanted to be humiliated. He took Steve back to his camper truck and asked to be tied up with his top-sider laces. "Bite my balls till they bleed!" is the line I remember our laughing about most.

I woke Thursday morning curled against Robbie and already rubbing my cock up and down the crack of his ass, which was still slick. Soon he stopped pretending to be asleep and reached around and started jerking me off. As I was gey-sering over Robbie's pumping fist, Steve strolled up looking for his cigarettes, on his way to drive Randy to Carmel for work.

1984

February 28, 1984

I've been rereading "Nantucket Diary" and "Being Alone" from the last Rorem collection: Ned at fifty-five, fussy, through with sex, also drink. "My name is Ozymandias, King of Kings: look on my works, ye mighty, and despair!"

Steve was in town for the weekend, up for a Napa wine rep function on Saturday. He arrived late and spent Friday night; was already back from Napa when I got off work Saturday. We drank a glass of wine and went to Hamburger Mary's for dinner, where a cute waiter who's certainly seen me there before without batting an eye, placed his crotch against my shoulder and hissed at a hunky busboy who smiled at me, "I saw him first!" By the time we'd emptied a carafe Steve went into the "there could have been something more between us, but you didn't want that" refrain he dredges up now and then when we're drunk and sans Randy. The truth is that starting with the time he took me home to bed my first week at Bonanza, fucked me till 2:00 A.M. and then kicked me out in the rain and let me find my way home from Nob Hill to Noe and Eighteenth, he'd made it clear we were to be carousing buddies only. But now he likes the Disney version. "I love you, I really do you know."

Several bars later and a $40 ticket on Polk Street for making a U-turn to nab a parking place, we walked into 20 Monroe and fell to fucking nastily without preamble.

I love Steve's cock. I really do, you know. It's such a pretty, unusual-looking uncut one—not a lot of foreskin, and a distinctive sort of pale band that I always insist is where they started to circumcise him, but changed their minds—and it stays so hard. He fucked me every which way, let me fuck him, fucked me again till he came. We woke erect and moving against each other in the early morning, and he fucked me long and vigorously then, and came in me. We lay panting and wet; he smoked a cigarette and I waited for him to signal our return to normal "friends" footing. *That's that*, I thought. He mentioned "that year you were mad at me," and I lay there all fucked out and laughing and said, "You're right, Steve, I was stubborn and wrong and the only way to settle this once and for all is for you to just fuck me as cruel and rough and selfish as you can…" I was half-teasing, but his cock zipped up his pelvis to his belly button like a sweep second hand and he shoved it in again and fucked me violently for another twenty minutes, then pulled out and straddled my chest jerking off while I sucked his balls and jerked myself off till I shot for the first time in all this in several big jets that hit him in the back of the head and ran down his shoulders and he said, "Wow."

On Tuesday I got an emotional letter from him, written after he'd gotten home Sunday afternoon. I felt a pang as I read; I could tell he was very aware that I might ridicule or discount what he'd written (*If I could go back to a feeling forever, it would be that one*). I know it's no marriage proposal, and we'll probably never discuss it again, but something happened that kind of shook us both, I think.

March 4, 1984

People always want to make you feel as though you've missed the best, some incommunicable belle epoch that passed away just before you'd rounded the corner. Like Steve used to go on about the summer of '77 on Polk Street, till his eyes grew misty over gone Quaaludes and he'd fumble in his glove compartment for a Zomax. Because of my capacity for believing in the nostalgia of others, life had always seemed to me like a party arrived at late, all the interesting men drunk or gone home with someone else.

I wrote the above paragraph on a notepad at work last summer, thinking I was about to begin the short story I used to write in my head whenever I drank too much coffee on a hangover, the Sam story, the story of the end of wantonness— or at least the possibility of it—with the coming of AIDS. This, because Gary walked in and announced one day in his patronizing way he'd got a great title for a story I could write—as if to say, here, I've done all the work, you can fill in the rest, it's a gift: Death Comes to Town. All I could think was that I'd heard it somewhere before.

It's a sunny day; I'm going out for the first time this year in my gray OP shorts, with Gina.

March 16, 1984

Wasn't it right about the time I stopped feeling suicidal that I examined my life and found it worthless? I wrote this in a letter to Buddy the other day, and was awfully well pleased with myself. Copying it out now I only feel it's silly melodrama, the unromantic fact of a whine. I'm far too terrified of sickness to be even allusively suicidal.

Steve called and woke me at 10:30 this morning and talked at me for an hour. Will he and Randy actually move apart? I still don't quite believe it. Steve's seeing a Freudian psych from Estonia: "Separate your mind and body, put your emotions aside and use your intellect for the next few months...." Sounds a strain to me. Steve's having an affair with the guy who cuts his hair: Does that qualify?

Antsy and horny, I walked to the Magazine and chatted with Bob (ignoring the *Be Brief* sign atop the cash register); bought a dirty mag: *Campus Cocks*. Drinking a Calistoga at Polk Gulch, I picked up a *BAR* and read a front page story about an older gay businessman who'd been murdered by the marine he picked up. The victim was bashed to death with a table leg, his eyeballs exploded and face detached from the skull. The marine's being championed by the small Georgia town he comes from. This makes me think: Mom's been remiss with her clipping service lately, or have there just been fewer sad middle-aged gay men stabbed to death by young Latino trade in El Paso this year?

I might have tricked Saturday night, but threw him back after the gratification of a catch. I'd just bought my first drink at Giraffe when I noticed a hyper, slim guy with a dark, close-ly-trimmed beard, nattily dressed in white shirt, tie, and tan slacks, staring hard at me, as far as I could tell from the few yards' distance (my glasses were, of course, in my coat pocket). I smiled in the general direction of his face and he charged over and asked if he could buy me a drink. "Sure, c'mon over and talk to me," I said, and he did, irritating me a bit by backing my stool into the corner and slapping a leg across one of mine. At the same time I noticed crooked, crowded teeth and a sour breath. *I can't kiss this person*, I thought, and despite his prom-ising body I began plotting my escape. Still, I was of two minds about "Rod"—("Oh, short for Roderick?" I'd asked, trying to give him airs of Usher. "No, *Rodney*," he said, eyeing me sus-piciously, as though I might turn out to be slightly off). He looked like he'd be energetic in bed, either a fucker or an enthu-siastic fuckee. Actually, when I declined to go home with him as we walked out at last call, citing "health concerns" (which probably wouldn't have stopped me if I'd really wanted to go with him), he informed me huffily, "I don't get fucked and I don't fuck. I just meant a mutual jack-off session!" I voiced what I at least half believe these days—I don't want to fuck with someone without at least a second sober meeting.

"Oh, you mean like date for six months and then maybe you'll fuck?" he said in a decidedly nasty tone. I put out my hand as if to say no hard feelings, but he glared at me and stormed off toward his South of Market home.

From that chamber, and from that mansion, I fled aghast.

April 7, 1984

Friday night drinks after work with Louise, the smart and funny Scottish girl who's come to work at the store and red-haired Martha, her friend who's just been hired as well, upstairs at Hoffman's. ("You and your little snotty sorority," John groused one day, assuming we talk about him, so I've dubbed us Sigma Snipe.) Then I dashed home for a quick joint and set off for the Gulch, where I sipped beers till eleven. A very tall and inebriated Indian guy from Oklahoma pawed me, trying to drag me home to his lover ("He's from Texas, like you!") and attempting to estimate my crotch ("How many inches you got, anyways?"). A terribly fucked up little queen danced with himself in the doorway, eliciting horn blasts and shouts from passing traffic, and occasionally uttering non sequiturs like "Get over it!" to no one in particular.

April 25, 1984

Unpleasantness at work over my refusal to put on one of the black grocer's aprons John's bought for us and stand out on the sidewalk for two hours trying to sell books to people who might not otherwise come into the store on their lunch. (This marketing brainstorm hasn't met with much success since the paperbacks fade, curl, and grow filthy from the Market Street grime in half an hour, but putting on the apron's become the Oath of Allegiance in the new world order.) The atmosphere's been strained on and off since John's become "boss." So I've taken today and tomorrow off to look for a new job.

This morning I showered and dressed in what passes for my best (black jeans instead of blue), headed to L&S Distributors for my meeting with the owner, whom I'd never met before, but have long heard of. I was shown up to his dusty office above the warehouse space on Post Street. While we talked he kept stopping to punch in one ringing or buzzing phone line after another, then turned these huge, baby-bird-like brown eyes back to me, his body cocked oddly like a bird's, due to some chronic problem I'd been told about beforehand. He'd whip up close to his desk/command center in his extremely mobile rolling desk chair, then come scooting all knees and goggle-eyes over to me till I wondered if he'd halt before we became entangled. He offered me a job right away as a "paper runner," zipping

newspapers around town in a truck in the middle of the
night, which he seemed pretty sure I'd decline, and I did.
"And you *don't* want to be a rep, ah-hmmm," he said, tap-
ping his nose with a finger. I explained I hoped to work in
the warehouse whenever an opening might occur (I'd been
told by someone who knows that there is one coming up).
He skidded up to me so that our knees met, darting his eyes
in either direction as if the walls had ears, and stage whispered, "But those guys *never leave!*"

Next I hit Clean Well-Lighted Place, where I was given a
standard job application form identical to what one would be
handed at Taco Bell, and a depressing quiz ("name three
works by Virginia Woolf"). Then Green Apple Books, where
they say the manager's a total witch, and little, creaky-floored
Browser Books on Fillmore.

Yesterday, a tense forty-five minute discussion with John
in the shipping room, then out to lunch with Gina. I walked
back in to man the registers with Martha, and as we stood
gossiping about Anita Brookner's *Look at Me*, the light fix-
tures jarred and rattled noisily and forty-year-old dust bunnies
wafted down and a customer writing a check paused and held
up the pen as if it were a barometer and said, "I believe we're
having an earthquake." The floor rolled impressively twice, in
two long, swaying jerks and Martha and I just stared at each
other. Six-point-two and centered in San Jose, the radio said.

May 27, 1984

Just finished Elizabeth Jane Howard's *After Julius*. A character in it says what everybody's really looking for is another person to see them exactly as they would be seen. Every time I've approximated love, I've been delirious with feeling like the person I *would* be, if only the right person loved me. I still refuse to consider that it might never properly come; I'm twenty-eight, OK, that's getting older, but there's still lots of time, isn't there?

Thursday, I left the store with Louise to meet her husband Johnny at Jerry and Johnny's. We sat in a rickety booth in the run-down, Hammett-era newspaper bar, drinking vodka-grapefruits. It was pretty empty but for some old crows cackling at one end of the long bar, and two extremely hunky construction workers in the booth behind ours. I had my eye on one of them every second I deemed it safe (he wasn't facing us)—slim, but very muscular, wearing faded Levis that stretched tightly around his hard butt and big thighs. I was too dim to notice what Louise had without even staring: the two were having an argument that abruptly escalated into a fight. Hardly any blows landed; it was all straining muscles, jumping veins, and white fingerprints on their flushed, red flesh where they'd tried to pull each other's faces off. My man was gripped in a headlock in seconds. We were flattened back in our booth to avoid flying fists and elbows, Johnny saying, "OK guys, it's a draw, have another drink...." Louise slapped my leg, seeing me gawking at the quivering, muscular ass three feet away, legs slightly spread, pinned bent over by his adversary.

Can it possibly be that the chimes I hear just now wafting from Grace Cathedral are playing "I Left My Heart in San Francisco"?

July 4, 1984
Stayed out last night sleeping over with goateed, heavy-set Seth, with whom I'd been flirting over the past week when I'd run into him in the pathetically named Company on Nob Hill. I fell from my boring plateau of disease avoidance by degrees. I only meant to be chatting with him, buying each other drinks; then I really only meant to share my joint with him at his place just down the block. We sat and talked and drank beer till 3:30, when I rose to leave, pleased with my good judgment, and we hugged good-bye—but then we were nuzzling each other's faces and then we both had erections and that was that.

He was nice but sort of childish-acting; I hadn't really gotten a sexual fix on him other than that he seemed determined to get me home with him. His dick was smallish, but hard, and he was very horny. He wanted me to fuck him after a while, which I was pleased to do, climbing atop his plump ass and slipping in easily. I yanked out when I came ("Why'd you do that?") and then let him jack off straddling my face. When I went to leave in the morning we hugged at the door—I was dressed, he had on a bathrobe—and we both got hard-ons and I decided what the fuck, and got down on my knees and sucked him off for real.

July 28, 1984

Tiredness at very little sleep last night is beginning to catch up with me, but I'm still elated at tricking with a handsome, clever, and very horny British guy last night. How good it felt, getting up to pee or wash and knowing there'd be this funny, good-looking stud waiting to put his arms around me when I climbed back into bed.

I'd gone out late, after reading all evening; put on faded blue corduroy pants, black high tops, and new gray pinstriped shirt, and walked down the hill to Giraffe. When I turned around, drink in hand, to figure out where to station myself in the crowded bar, I saw an empty stool opposite me, next to some people around a table. The guy nearest, whom I hadn't dared to look at, said, "Hello, how are you?" in a cute English accent and smiled broadly. He looked like photos of Joe Orton in the John Lahr biography: short-cropped light hair, big blue eyes, boyish, pale face with a broad nose; a short, muscular body clad in Levi's, T-shirt and high tops. He shifted right around on his stool and started peppering me with questions. His name is Arno Duras, which sounds like a thug in an early

Hitchcock thriller. Not quite: he's a flight steward for British Airways, in town on a thirty-six-hour layover; hasn't been here since 1980, has a lover in Sussex; thought I had the cutest eyes he'd ever seen.

As we were talking, a fight broke out a few feet in front of us, and the tall, extremely handsome bartender who's been there for years, vaulted neatly over the bar and subdued the drunk who'd been bitch-slapping and shoving someone, propelling him by the collar to the swinging doors and out onto the street, just like on *Gunsmoke*. The atmosphere was strange for a few minutes; people seemed to be deciding whether they could return to laughing and drinking without endangering themselves, or whether the ejected one might burst back through the doors and spray the place with bullets.

After one neglected drink I asked Arno, who'd had his leg pasted to mine and was looking at me like he'd found a hundred dollar bill on the sidewalk, if he'd like to come back to my place and play. "No, but I was rather hoping you'd come back to my hotel room and play," he said. I was blissful, and becoming more aware of the nicely-muscled body beneath the clothes, not least the obvious bulge at his denimed crotch. And there was that gorgeous accent, not always understandable, and so attractively belligerent. We walked over to the Van Ness Holiday Inn, Arno making fun of my stride and running in little Chaplinesque shuffles to keep up. I felt some shyness returning as I realized I was about to climb into bed with this almost intimidatingly hunky stranger. I gave him big points for grabbing me the second the door to his room shut behind us. I thought it was endearing that he drew the drapes (we were on the twenty-fourth floor) and flicked on the TV with the sound off. We returned to kissing, hands on each other's asses. He reached for my cock first; it was poking straight up and just over the top of my belt. He pushed me back at arm's length and said, "Here, let's get this off then," and unbuttoned my shirt and I couldn't just stand there any longer and started wrestling off my shoes, jeans, and socks, staring back at him. "Now you," I said, and lay back on the bed with an arm across my forehead, half-watching till he got to some blue bikini underwear, from which protruded something very large. He smiled, hooked his fingers in the elastic, and yanked the jockey's down, and a beautiful, very thick, uncut cock bounded out. I may have actually cheered.

We kissed and wrestled around in that first incredible jolt of hard, naked flesh against your own. I'd forgotten how much more intense this is when it's a body and a face—a person—you aren't making allowances for; when you want to press every inch of flesh up against every corresponding inch of him, Peter reclaiming his strayed shadow.

The sex was both smutty and sweet, lots of kissing, lots of mutual cocksucking; I came once with him just beginning to enter me; I couldn't really take it any further. What felt best, and what this cocky, butch, cockney-accented delinquent seemed most to like was my fucking his perfect, hard ass. I fucked him twice in the course of the night, and again in the morning. "You're my little fuckbox then, aren't you?" he said.

August 12, 1984
Walking back up Pine Street after dinner on Polk last night, I coaxed Gina into the Gate for a nightcap. Straight Isn't the Gate: it's gay, but it's also one of those odd little neighborhood alcoholic bars with a regular cast of aging or downright elderly serious drinkers seated in their customary places around the long, rectangular counter like the celebrities on *Hollywood Squares*, and the occasional guest appearance by curious tourists stumbling up or down the hill from their hotels.

We took the only two empty stools and hadn't been there long before a very cute, slightly drunk guy on the opposite side of Gina—my age, possibly younger, short, with a trim, sexy build ("Doesn't he remind you of Gary?" she whispered)— turned around and started talking to us. He lived nearby, he said, and had walked by here many times, always meaning to come in sometime for a drink. Now his girlfriend was out of town for the weekend and he was tired of staring at the walls, so here he was. "You two a couple?" Not exactly. "We're 'Two On a Party,'" Gina said, smiling. We'd just been reminiscing about the Tennessee Williams story by that name, or rather, Gina had been dredging up our favorite lines, about Cora and Billy and their adventures picking up sailors together in bars. ("Sometime, said Cora, you're going to get off the party.... If I get off the party, we'll get off it together, said Billy. And me do *what*? She'd ask him, realistically.") Our new little friend (he never said his name) hitched his stool up closer. "Sometimes I think about experimenting with another guy, you know? Like a three-way, two guys with a chick. You ever try that?" Some Chablis went down my windpipe and I coughed, elbowing Gina's little felt cloche hat off the bar.

"Let me," he said, sliding off his stool and dropping on all fours. He took his time finding the hat, while Gina and I looked at each other quizzically. Had literature come to life? His flushed face surfaced at knee level, and he inhaled crudely in the general direction of Gina's lap. "Ummm."

He went on asking probing questions and making wistful, suggestive remarks about his pent-up sex drive while never quite making an unmistakable pass, and we were both too wary of his inebriation to boldly ask him home for a drink or joint—so this adventure went no further. Several cocktails later, he slid off his stool and staggered out without fulfilling his fantasy, or ours.

"Tell me why we won't regret this the rest of our lives," I said.

"I like you the way that a cattleman loves a sheepherder!" Gina said, quoting Williams's thick-necked trade who turns ugly, and we laughed.

August 26, 1984
Adventures in dreamland only: last night, Saturday, I smoked a joint thinking that, pleasantly stoned, I'd put music on, shave, shower, dress, and walk to Polk. What a money-saver a little joint may be! I lay on the rug listening to music, jerked off, drank a quart of milk, watched the news (three deadly plane crashes, Truman Capote dead at fifty-nine, controversy over government suggestion that AIDS patients be put on national list for blood banks) and went to sleep by 11:30.

Sunday morning, the last of August; next week will be September, and while September and October here are often the sunniest months, there's still that twinge at the arrival of fall. I don't think, *well, another week gone by and I haven't fallen in love,* or *gee, another visit to the dentist and I still haven't got a lover*—but now it comes like a silent film title and hangs heavy over my head: another summer gone, and I haven't fallen in love. No-nonsense Louise would make a good editor for me, jotting here in the margin, "Shut it, Kevin!" or "Don't be daft."

A year soon, since I stopped seeing Gary. Last week, looking for a phone number in a little cubbyhole I stick scraps of paper into above my desk at work, I found the note Michael jotted when he came by to say good-bye before moving back to Florida and missed me. I haven't heard from him since.

September 2, 1984
Friday I got my hair cut short over Martha's and Louise's objections ("But I'm not trying to attract straight girls," I said), then went with them after work to Temple Bar for drinks and dish, Gina joining us later. Earlier, I'd picked up vacation prints from Gina's and my week in Guerneville, into which I'd slipped the old negative of a photo of Sam I used to moon over, then burnt years back in an uncharacteristic venture into ritual.

Looking at that print now, I have the same curious and guilty feeling I used to have when I'd bury a dead pet turtle and then dig it up months later to check on history at work. The change most apparent here: while I used to stare and stare and see only Sam, now, after a cursory glance at a stranger with a silly wild West mustache and a shifty, half-tolerating expression, I see only me, pathetically clinging to this skinny guy who's already slipping out of my arms. I look like a baby monkey in a Jane Goodall documentary. I thought the look on my face was one of slavish devotion; Gina says I look horribly unhappy.

September 17, 1984
Friday I met Louise and Martha at Sutter's Mill for drinks,

then we continued to Jerry and Johhny's. On one journey up the creaking stairs to the restroom I picked up a hammer lying on the ground and chipped away the plaster to erase the ancient, scrawled "FAGS" off the wall between the Men's and Women's doors.

Saturday I bought two new pairs of cords, brown and black. Nate came by later and we smoked several joints and headed to Polk and the Giraffe, where we sat at a table and made each other laugh through a number of beers and vodka grapes, certain we were the hottest things this side of Adonis the bartender. "Tell the truth," I asked Nate of my snug new brown cords. "Are these pants too tight?"

"Oh, are you wearing pants?"

September 18, 1984

I was taken aback to see a zaftig Nick Pargetter browsing the bargain book tables at the store yesterday. Has he forgotten I work there? I rushed to the back and busied myself unpacking a bunch of crappy mass-market paperbacks (romances, science fiction; sinking-ship, hijacked-plane or harvested-organs pot-boiler of the month).

Nick was my first real San Francisco boyfriend. He was thirty-seven and already stout in the fall of '77, but I imagined he looked like Alan Bates, or like one of my adolescent friends' attractive fathers who'd step in during a sleepover to say "Stop horsing around now, boys" in a pair of bulging Jockey shorts—with his thickly-furred torso, and that nice red cock jutting out from under his stomach. He chain-smoked cigarettes and dope, wheezed, coughed up mucous constantly, and mouthed a pocket handkerchief à la Camille, but oh that sexy, hoarse voice: "Now look here, handsome, do you want to *be* with me tonight, or what?" ("Being" meant getting fucked in the ass and then listening to Nick snore.) He was big and physically warm, if emotionally an est-ravaged tundra, and he lived in a creaky little Victorian house in Noe Valley with a big cat named Toker who came and went through a broken basement window, growling noisily.

The small two-story house, while nicely painted and full of great old Victorian couches and lamps, was dusty and in disarray, half-full coffee cups left on side tables for weeks before a big wash-up. There weren't any curio cabinets, track lights, or flower arrangements. At the top of the echoing, uncarpeted stairs, on a dusty maroon wall, was a huge, somewhat amateur, movie prop-like portrait of a striking young man, left behind with the possessions of an artist friend who'd O.D.'d in the sixties.

I house sat for him one weekend that November while he went camping "alone" on some family land in Marin County, and I was stupidly surprised when I read the postcard he left propped up on his bedside table a week later—from a little friend thanking him for the great weekend and "especially the really loving sex." There were tears, and the first of a frustrating series of discussions about what was supposed to be going on between us; this was when I glimpsed the sawdust behind the Alan Bates mask. For the month or two we continued to see each other I became completely cynical about him; where before, I'd been childishly "in love," careful not to cross or offend him, after my disappointment I felt in control, pleased to be getting what I wanted from him in bed, and scorning him for a fool behind his back.

December 8, 1984
Listening to the new Psychedelic Furs album all week, making it the soundtrack to the pleasant days and nights I've spent with Arno the airhost since he called up Sunday evening, back just as he said he'd be when we met last July.

He's charming, boyish, and handsome—that hasn't changed. Yes, he has a lover and an existence halfway across the world; fine. I haven't got anyone right now, and this is nice, and while I can't help being delighted to see him I don't feel sad or anxious or in love. "Did you miss me, then?" he asks often. "Did you miss *me?*" I counter—at home with his other half? 'Course not.

He was here Sunday night to Wednesday morning, then back last night. I was summoned to the Holiday Inn last

evening; he'd been lying in bed napping, in his little striped
Jockeys. I dragged them down to his knees and stuck it in
doggy-style, with him crouched at the foot of the huge hotel
bed, his ass so tight it scraped my dick.

After sex, we're lying in bed panting but otherwise silent;
then, Arno props his head on one arm and asks, as if he were
Greer Garson, and I'd just returned from the war: "Have I
changed much then?"

"Since Wednesday?" I asked.

John says I've become a cold fish.

1985

January 29, 1985

Last Thursday night I stayed up very late speed-reading Carroll Baker's ludicrous autobiography, *Baby Doll*, in preparation for my much-anticipated lunch with her the next day. (The best passage is where she reluctantly loses her virginity to an older man on a train whose noises during sex she describes as "more of a gnnaarrrrr!") Walter, the sales rep escorting her around on her publicity stop here, had called the day before to tell me where to show, a place called Gold Street Bar and Grill on the little Barbary Coast alley way out Montgomery. There were maybe eight other bookstore people present: Dick from L&S, Dante from Paperback Traffic. High-decibel Walter herded us upstairs, pulled out a chair for the movie star, then began seating us very specifically, "You there, you there..." I'd expected to gawk at the guest of honor from way down the table, but he generously put me right beside her. She was very nice, playing gracious lady and acting like we knew as much about fancy Italian wines as she does—she ordered several bottles in that tremulous, hysteria-edged voice—talking mainly about food and restaurants in London and Rome (where she's been living). She looked amazingly well at fifty-two:

unlined Baby Doll china face intact, but for a slight double chin. I told her when other kids on our block were playing Tarzan on the swing set, I was pretending to be her in *The Carpetbaggers*, swinging scantily clad from the chandelier. "How nice, dear," she said.

All the waiter boys kept finding reasons to come over and pour water or top off our wine to get closer to her. Our waiter was an adorable Irish boy who kept winking and grinning at me and passing little sexy remarks as he leaned over to serve.

My interest in her was all based on having seen *Baby Doll* for the first time last year and being really surprised at how good she was, but I couldn't just elbow her in the ribs and say, "Enough about Rome, I want to hear all about playing *Baby Doll!*" *Gnnaarrr!*

February 19, 1985

I've just finished reading *Bad Sister* by Emma Tennant. Interesting: Jane is told to call the Satan figure in her visions Gil-Martin, or "K"—"a bent line that comes in on a straight line and shoots it to pieces." When I was being expelled for several days during my senior year following the ill-advised "Satan Poster" stunt (I and several fellow malcontents plastered the decorated Homecoming halls with a crude parody of the ubiquitous Jesus festival broadsides), the humorless ex-coach principal (whose yearbook photo we had pasted onto

Satan) told me, "Your trouble is you're a smart boy but you've always been a bit bent in the wrong direction."

March 4, 1985

I thought of Bernie Moreau for no reason this morning. He was just a guy I tricked with one Saturday night at the 'N Touch and then saw for a couple of weeks after that in the winter of '78: mid-thirties, nice body, dark-skinned, curly black hair, and hairy all over; divorced, with teenage kids living elsewhere. He was always very kind to me, though there was never any suggestion of romance on either side. I thought of him as a bit old and eccentric, though he was very good looking. He'd take me to his studio on Leavenworth, light a candle up in his little loft bed, strip me and have me lay spread-eagled on my stomach while he rubbed baby oil meticulously over every inch of me, paying fanatical attention to my butt, kneading, probing, licking, then really chowing down, putting his tongue as far up me as he could, breathing into me: all very relaxing and arousing. Finally he'd stick his fat, hard uncut dick into me (he'd push my hands back over my head if I tried to reach around and touch it before then) and fuck me long and slow—then he'd flip me over and suck my cock till I shot like crazy.

He dropped me flat at some point when I was just getting used to his little regimen, saying he'd got a lover—but I saw him out cruising at the 'N Touch most weekends after that, and he was always polite, but clearly had eaten his fill of my twenty-two-year-old ass.

March 5, 1985

Last week, returning a movie to Captain Video after work, I stopped for some cocktails at the Detour, which was fairly deserted. Watched two butch clones play pool, then left while I still felt pleased with the appraising glances I'd gotten, before the creepy-looking guy in the shadows behind the chain-link fence could come up and depress me.

When I stepped into the MUNI underground car I noticed the handicapped girl right away, her complicated electric wheelchair backed up to the opposite door. She was hunched up over a sheaf of papers, her hair elaborately done up in a country singer cascade of corkscrew curls, perky bow on one side. (I thought of Mary Kay Place as Loretta Haggers, the would-be country singer on *Mary Hartman, Mary Hartman*, who was, for a few episodes, paralyzed.) There were only two other riders, both gay, one just across from me looking out the window at the walls going by, chin in hand. As the crippled girl apparently reached the end of the page she was reading and began pawing at the paper with a tiny, clawish hand, the guy, without really looking, shot over, turned the page, and sat down again. *Sweet*, I thought. We jerked into the next stop and both men got off. I was alone with her. Sure enough, she began pawing the page moments later.

"Can I get that for you?" I said. She produced some unpleasant and undeniably negative sounds, and began irritably batting at the page. As in a cartoon, a huge staple shot from the corner and all the pages sprang out across the floor and under seats. I jumped up, gathered all I could find, shuffled them back into a neat pile, and approached her, saying stupidly, "What page were you on?" She swung her face around at me, mouthing unintelligibly, white stuff at the corners of her lips. It seemed like maybe she wanted me to stow the papers in her open backpack, so I did. She continued to gesticulate in a way that convinced me she wanted moving in some way. I wrenched her locked chair around to face the door, and we came into Powell Street station. "Is this your stop? Do you want off here?" She got nasty again, flailing about; I felt she could be loosely interpreted as saying, "You idiot, get away from me!"

"Bye now," I said, feeling tearful. The driver was emerging from behind his partition at the front of the car as I got out. "Hey, wait a minute!" he yelled.

"Not her stop!" I said, waving, and took the stairs by threes, wondering if she'd be giving the police a composite portrait of me an hour from now.

March 24, 1985
Call from Steve at work Friday, after not hearing from him for

some time—the saga continues. His current affair: "He's not my type at all, big, six-foot-one, dark; well, he's Italian! Full beard, you know I don't like beards!"

"Oh, what's he do?"

"Haha, well—he owns his own—Well, go ahead and laugh, he's a hair stylist"—(I screamed and customers eyed the office window)—"but he's real butch. And he's nice, really nice, I think we might be heading for a living-together relationship...."

April 7, 1985

Up for an hour reading *Sister Carrie* in the nice new Penguin edition, putting the book aside now and again to indulge in unfounded fantasies about the interesting-looking friend of Sandra's I saw two weeks ago when he came by work to meet her. Dark-haired, hunky-looking. I asked Sandra yesterday (we work a Saturday morning together every two weeks), "*Who was that?*"

"What? My friend Todd? I've told you about him. You think he's cute?"

"Yeah."

"That's funny, he was asking about you."

April 18, 1985

The Todd Story: of what duration I don't yet know. I met him, with Gina and Sandra, at the Cedar on Friday for *Baby Doll*, which he and Sandra hadn't seen. I liked his looks, but right off I had misgivings about what he was saying, and at what volume. I was embarrassed. We went for pizza afterward, soon splitting off into two conversations: Sandra and Gina, poetry; Todd and myself, boyfriends, safe sex, lack of sex, his gym program (fairly apparent), snatches of personal history. He drove us by Monroe, asked could he call me up; I said sure, thinking I ought to know better.

He called Sunday morning and said, "Can I ask you something personal—Did you used to know a person named Ray Barone?" I was suitably shocked. "I'm afraid so. Why do you ask?"

"Well, I went out with him for a couple of months about a year ago, and he used to talk about someone named Kevin all the time, and I just figured out who you were."

He came over later that day and we went up on the roof to sunbathe. He told his Ray story, I mine. After they'd broken up, Ray had stalked him for months, at one point breaking the antenna off Todd's car. "What about your door buzzer?" I asked. Todd had brought along a loaf of bread and peanut butter and he ate thickly spread slices while he talked. I applied some tanning cream to his back.

"Do you think we could have a sexual relationship?" he asked, deadpan.

"I'd expected we'd try," I said.

He sort of sidled up to me and threw an arm over my back and began to rub my ass. I turned my head and we kissed a bit, impeded somewhat by the peanut butter. I got a hard-on all the same and suggested we go downstairs. We lay on my bed and kissed and hugged a while. It was nice enough, in an anonymously good-willed way. I liked his chest hair. Then we pulled off our shorts and got down to some Safe Sex, jerking each other off, sucking balls, sniffing around; exciting enough, given my recent hibernation. He roared affectedly at climax, which sent me into paroxysms of self-consciousness neighbor-wise. We definitely operate on different noise levels.

May 4, 1985
Good week, sweetened by relief: I called Todd and blew off our getting together Tuesday night. After the last evening we'd spent together, I knew I could never consider him anything but an idiot. Why oh why did I go out with him even once, having realized he was a dope that first evening? I thought somehow the sex might be good enough to make the rest of him bearable; it wasn't. He was annoyingly himself during it, accusing me of looking glazed-eyed, as if I were somewhere else (trying!), stage directing me to suck his inert nipples, moaning loudly in a fakey fashion that would make a cat laugh. He was neurotic about his tiny nose, and you couldn't blame him, though it was the least of my problems with him. He's had a number of

plastic surgeries after a childhood car accident, and still isn't happy with the current result. Yet he was handsome in a crazed looking way, with dark hair swooping up in a sort of Elvis pompadour, like one of the gang from *Archie and Veronica*.

Last Wednesday, while I made snapper, broccoli, and potatoes, he lay on the bed yammering boorishly about how long I might take fixing the meal, how late we'd be eating, how he hates eating at nine o'clock. Over dinner there was an unpleasant conflict over the pronunciation of "flaccid." He asked if I'd like him to dress real sexy, walk around in leather chaps. "Which?" I said. "I don't think chaps are sexy and the sort of guys who go around in them usually strike me as likely to be flaccid with their pants off."

"Many people make the mistake you just made," he said obnoxiously. "Actually, it's 'flak-cid.' I grabbed a paperback dictionary and looked it up, and was appalled to find his odd pronunciation confirmed, with no alternate listing. (A later search in a newer *Webster's* at Bonanza yielded my version as the first of two choices.) "Don't be embarrassed," he said. "I had a well-educated uncle who'd always say 'mizzled' instead of 'misled.'" At this moment, I wanted to take another crack at his nose with a piece of flatware.

July 6, 1985
After several beery discussions of tensions at Bonanza and the

impending departure of Martha's co-worker at Minerva's Owl, the thing is done; I gave notice I'd be gone at the end of the month, and now I've already become accustomed to getting up earlier and down to Levi Plaza to open the tiny shop there at 8:30 A.M.

"You're being peremptory and a bit neurotic!" John poked his head into the shipping room to deliver this last shot, because I'd declined a farewell lunch. In our first days at Bonanza eight years ago, John was at odds with an older, fussy, fiftyish gay man, Marvin, who wore a blazer every day, was always ducking into the shipping room to break open a vitamin E capsule and massage the goo under his eyes, studied Flamenco, and badmouthed us behind our backs to Mrs. Eidenmueller. (To add to the eccentricity, we were required to call Marvin "Fred" in front of Mrs. Eidenmueller: her late husband, a tyrant, had been named Mervyn, and she didn't like to be reminded of him.) John always cited Marvin (Fred) as an example of "that sort of middle-aged, frustrated, neurotic gay man." Now, no doubt, I've entered the pantheon of psycho fags.

July 28, 1985
Walking home from Minerva's Owl Books Thursday I almost turned down Bush to Sutter's Mill for a drink, feeling cocky in a new pair of jeans, but opted to head home and finish the Edna O'Brien I've been enjoying, *The Country Girls*. The

phone was ringing as I walked in: Arno back, two days shy of a year since our first meeting. I cleaned up and raced over to that monolithic Holiday Inn on Van Ness. He opened the door clad in blue briefs and a gold chain, with his boyish cropped hair, and the bluest eyes I've ever seen. "You look older," he said, holding me at arm's length a moment, "No, more mature. A mustache suits you. You're still my old fuckbox then, aren't you?" I fell on him at once; he resisted ("Let's talk a bit first; let's go eat something") but his huge dick was hard. I wrestled one of the pocketful of rubbers I'd brought along onto my cock, bent him over his open suitcase at the foot of the bed, and, with some hand lotion grabbed from his shaving kit (knocking over the stuffed "I love you *this* much" huggy bears on the vanity), slid my boner into his pretty ass and fucked him vigorously, reaching around to jack him off so that we came together. After the weeklong headline blitz about Rock Hudson and AIDS, I was determined to keep safe. Arno was bemused at my eccentricity: "What's this then? So it's rubbers, is it? That's so American..."

We went out for pizza at Victor's; he rattled on—"I've chucked my lover. I have two Australian boyfriends now. They talk like real men—they look straight, see? I want an Australian lover. Well then, you can't blame me, can you?" I registered this as offensive, but laughed it off.

Friday evening I hiked over again, optimistically stopping

at Headlines to pick up six lubed condoms. I was full of next-day lust, ready to tear off his jeans and stick it in in a hurry, and I actually had his pants down before he successfully resisted: "Down horsie! We're going across the way for a drink with Linda!" This meant sitting in another air-conditioned hotel room that smelled of face cream and perfume drinking warm chablis out of a box, chatting aimlessly with a giddy stewardess in a caftan who stares at me with glassy eyes and drawls, "Fab!" or "Untrue!"

August 5, 1985
Something big has happened. I still think all those jerks who've assured me, "It'll happen, it'll come when you're least expecting it," are full of shit—Was it really necessary for me to wait eight years to be sufficiently unsuspecting? But it *has* come out of nowhere, and I suppose I have Arno to thank for his part in it.

A week ago Saturday I went out with Arno; sitting at the bar in Giraffe, he carried on such a flirtation with the muscle-bound bartender I've always thought of as Ferdinand the Bull ("When the Matador missed him, Ferdinand kissed him"), my humorous tolerance fizzled and I put down my drink, strolled home, and unplugged the phone.

The next day, which was to have been spent with Arno, I left the phone unplugged till well past his departure time, then went to the Castro in the late afternoon. I had a couple of drinks in different bars, then rode the underground to Civic Center and walked down Polk to Giraffe.

I sat on a stool with my drink, thinking I'd have this last one and then toddle up the hill to meet Gina for our usual Sunday night pizza and regale her with my latest war story. Sitting at the end of the bar was a tall, dark-haired, Italian? Jewish? guy, in black dress pants and a white shirt, his tie pulled off and tucked into his pocket—a waiter who'd just gotten off work? He was looking at me and smiling broadly, like he'd just come across an old friend. I literally looked either side of me and pointed sheepishly to my chest as if to say, "Me?"

I went over and sat beside him. We introduced ourselves— his name is Jack—and started talking easily. I'm not the only one who's just walked away from something; he's just quit his job as maître d' of some pricey new restaurant downtown. I kept thinking, *OK this guy's just really friendly, in a minute he'll drink up and say, "Nice talking to you," get up, and leave.* Does it only seem in retrospect that I already knew I was experiencing the thing we read about and watch in old movies— there's no getting around the corny phrase—love at first sight?

It was getting on time to meet Gina. "I could come along, if your friend wouldn't mind."

We met Gina at the Gate on Pine, then went to nearby Vito's for pizza. Jack charmed Gina while holding my knee under the table. Back here, more of that spooky, "something important is happening" feeling. When we pushed apart, got undressed, and lay down together on the bed, we just held each other and stared for a while. He's got a lovely broad-shouldered, mature body, thick mat of black chest hair on white skin, strong legs and thighs—he runs—a nice hard cock. We came the first time without penetration, just necking and clasping each other. It was as though we had to work past the shyness of the romantic feelings; each time we started kissing and got erect again, the sex got "dirtier." We came 69ing; I slid down onto his dick while we kissed and he fucked me roughly till, again, we came together. Though we'd discussed the concerns of the day—Rock's terrified and terrifying death-camp face bobbed along beside us up Bush Street, staring from every *Examiner* box—there was a tacit understanding that we were throwing in our lot together. We didn't mess with rubbers, then or since.

August 22, 1985

Last night was my first Jack-less since the fifth. I went out to dinner with Louise and Martha. Wandering up and down Grant Street in North Beach, I found a great old white fifties sports coat in a vintage clothing shop that fits me perfectly. I felt so happy walking down the street, tan and laughing in that white jacket, a smart, pretty woman either side of me. If I saw us from across the street I'd have said, let me be *him*. Something good has happened, and my friends are glad for me.

There must've been MSG in the miso soup at dinner; I woke from a nightmare later, scared shitless, unable to move. I'd been on a weird street crew—middle-aged women, office workers—trudging along a vast construction project, huge metal slabs loosely placed across shallow excavations. We each had to take a turn stepping onto one of the slabs and trying to rock it, to see if it was level. Mine wasn't. I felt with a sickening certainty what was going to come next. The slab was levered up: a corpse was underneath. I was to shift it about so that the slab would lie flat upon it.

I woke afraid and wishing Jack's big comforting body were there beside me.

November 24, 1985
It's been nearly two months since I handed 20 Monroe over to Martha to use as her art studio and moved into Jack's funky one bedroom in an old, carved up Pacific Heights mansion. The kitchen's a closet, but there are two working fireplaces, one taking up a whole wall of the wood-paneled bedroom.

Jack's got a new restaurant job managing down-at-heel Bruno's out in the Mission, a major comedown in the world for him, but he's not much bothered. Given our differing schedules five days a week, sex most often takes place when he comes in after midnight, smelling of pasta, wine, and cologne, yanking off his tie and shirt and wrestling me awake, his tongue in my mouth and a cold hand reaching for my cock. There's a dream-like quality to our fucking because I surface from a deep sleep and go back to it soon after.

Pleasant, relaxed Saturday yesterday: went to a movie, bought jeans and packages of new underwear since we were out by homely old Sears, went to dinner and held hands in the mainly straight couples crowd at Pizza Uno on Lombard. These date-type outings put my situation into happy perspective: Gee, I've got a handsome lover—how'd that happen?

The night before I moved in October, Michael Harper called from Florida—I hadn't heard from him in almost two years—to tell me Gary had died in August.

December 29, 1985

I was wakened at nine on this Sunday morning by a call from Buddy, now in New York: "I'm juggling two boyfriends right now. You know how easily I fall in love."

"Does this mean you're parking your lime-green Pinto in front of their houses?" I asked. (Ouida and Max had objected to Buddy's car remaining parked in front of the house all night when he and I were screwing back in '76.)

Christmas was very nice. We woke, lit fires in both rooms, opened our presents in bed. I'd rushed home from Minerva's the night before thinking, *What if I've imagined all this?* When

I walked in, Jack was already there and we kissed and held onto each other and I busted out crying because it is real, I'm happy, and I'm terrified of anything threatening it. To be held, to have him say "I know, I'm happy too,"—it was the best, the thing I'd schooled myself to stop expecting.

1986

February 1, 1986

Romantic morning with Jack. He instigated sex after one cup of coffee and the front section of the paper. It's always a happy surprise when he turns to me and wants to do it, when somehow I manage to look like I'm not breathlessly waiting for it. Because he's ten years older, he has the idea I'm up for it far more often than he is, and he informed me early on I couldn't just jump him every time I felt like it. For someone with plenty of past, he's got a funny prim side: when I picked up a porn video at the rental place, he objected. "I'm not going to watch that with you. You'll just expect me to have sex." In the end of course I put it on and very soon he lowered his book and stopped pretending he wasn't watching, and after about five minutes he smiled sheepishly and pulled down his sweats to expose his boner. "Don't let me pressure you," I said.

This morning, I jacked him off with us crouched facing each other, then jerked myself off with his cream, kissing all the while. Then, back to paper and book and espresso so strong I felt to be mildly tripping, and had a shiver of déjà vu about the afterglow, the paragraph I was reading, the quiet jazz on the radio, the heavy humidity between rainstorms.

Coming up the marble steps the other day I met Penny, the girl who lives in the other ersatz apartment on this floor. She calls Jack "Mr. Towel on the Right, Soap on the Left," having heard him yell those directions so frequently over the last five years to tricks hitting the shower that shares a thin wall (and very little water pressure) with hers.

I went down to the Giraffe to meet Jack when he got off work at his new job at Sutter 500 the other night. I carried a drink to my old roost in the front window, prepared to day-dream and gloat over no longer *having* to be there, but after only a moment a very drunk youngish guy was swaying in front of me, knocking my coat off the next stool, and blowing smoke in my face. "Hey! I see you just now and I say to myself, some people are living in fact and some are living in fiction, and baby, you are most definitely in fact! Fact—you are one handsome dude!" I stared at him, momentarily speechless. "Hey!"—Light shove to my shoulder—"I'm pay-ing you a compliment. Fact!"

Was he sent just to give me possibly the first opportunity in my life to confidently say, "I'm waiting for my boyfriend, actu-ally"? He spun away and attempted to punch open the heavy double Dutch doors to the sidewalk, which, unlatched in the middle, flapped in his face from four different angles, smashing the cigarette hanging out of his mouth in the most cartoon-like fashion, till he managed to pummel his way out amid laughter and comment from the bar. Ferdinand the Bull sashayed over like Mae West, collecting dead drinks on a cocktail tray. "I was about to toss him out for starting fights anyway."

March 1, 1986
Yesterday at Minerva's, as Martha and I stood at the register with our first lattes, she related the exciting details of her visit the previous evening to the new apartment of "Mr. Flavum," as we refer to her sexy, bad boy young suitor ("flavum" is some mythical substance like "flubber" he and his brother made up as adolescents; there's a tacit understanding on our part it refers to a particular bodily secretion). He'd been awaiting his chance to take her up on a certain blunt offer that had originally shocked his romantic sensibilities. Later in the morning, I relayed a call from her husband to her in the back of the store. Still later, darting to the back to pull a university press title from a teetering returns pile for one of our rare customers to browse, then drop on the counter and say "I'll see if Crown has it," I glimpsed Martha still on the phone and sobbing noisily, her face red and drenched. "Sorry!" I mouthed, and quickly backed out. After standing at the front of the store for twenty minutes feeling quite worried, certain her husband had found out about Mr. Flavum and was demanding an immediate divorce, I saw the light go out on the phone line. I waited a bit longer, then went back to find her mopping at her

face, hiding it when I came around the corner. "What's happened?" I asked.

"My mother's cat died!" she wailed, bursting into tears
again. I hugged her and beamed with relief over her shoulder.

1988

July 30, 1988

Three years ago today I smiled back at a handsome smiling man siting at the bar in Giraffe, and set in motion a different life. Now the events of the last six months are swimming away; when I think of something or pick up an object that suddenly brings him rushing back into focus, it's bad—in an instant I remember how beautiful and smart and funny he was, how brave he was about getting sick, how much he suffered, and there's all the tenderness, regret, and guilt over forgetting for a day.

1989

January 14, 1989

Sitting at Jack's desk, in that state of mind that's most often mine nowadays—not actively weeping, not happy—just robot-like, and wondering: If I'm very still can I avoid another bomb dropping on me? Thursday will be my thirty-third birthday. "Age" seems irrelevant: either I'll get sick and die in the next few years, or I won't.

I ran into Michael Harper's old roommate in the Emporium the other day. I knew what was coming from the look on his face when I asked if he'd heard from Michael lately. Michael's dead, as of last March. He'd been living in Florida. According to Jon, he freaked out over testing positive. He'd been having guilty nightmares about Gary, who'd say, "Why me, and not you?" (The spooky thing is, that's just what the Gary I knew *would* say.) So Michael borrowed a car and drove somewhere and shot himself.

I was just now remembering Michael, who'd been schooled in show tunes by the older men who picked him up as a mop-headed youth on Polk Street, breaking into a little tap dance and singing Cole Porter's "Too Darn Hot"as we walked down Bush to the bars on a rare warm summer night.

May 29, 1989

Sunning in the backyard, with Henry, the little dachshund we got six months before Jack died, snuffling around in the land-lord's overgrown vines and flowers. Beating off over a porn video this morning I suddenly recalled so clearly kissing Jack while I jerked off, when that was all he could do, yet he was still sexually involved, very into my coming. We'd kiss and kiss and I'd half think, am I breathing life into him, or sucking it out?

Over dinner last night, Bob and I argued about "happiness" in regard to my garbled quoting of these lines from Paul Bowles I'd read earlier: "I believe unhappiness should be studied very carefully; this is certainly no time for anyone to pretend to be happy, or to put his unhappiness away in the dark. (And anyone who is not unhappy now must be a monster, a saint, or an idiot.) You must watch your universe as it cracks above your head." Bob says you shouldn't expect to have happiness on more than a few occasions. I say, I was happy with Jack, and if I'm to live, I expect to find such a state again. Bob says finding Jack was essentially good luck, and isn't likely to happen twice. "You bitch," I said.

September 20 1989

This is the last morning of Bob's and my three days at Russian River, at the musty Village Inn in Monte Rio. The second night, Monday, we showered and went down to the bar for a pre-dinner drink, and I noticed a guy who seemed vaguely familiar to me. Then we took our drinks to the big parlor overlooking the river to play backgammon—and the familiar fellow followed us in and sat reading a paperback in a big, overstuffed chair. Bob and I realized neither of us actually remembered how to play; I impulsively turned to the guy with the book and asked if he knew. He was all smiles—that kind of tight, nervous smile Gary Reed had—and rushed to my side and leaned very closely to explain the play. I was looking at his nicely made, muscular, pale-haired forearms, when I felt a sort of thump in the pit of my stomach and realized who he was. He finished giving rules and sample plays, taking longer than necessary, and returned to his chair. I was going back to the bar for more drinks and asked if I could get him one for his trouble. As I walked out, he'd jumped up and was introducing himself to Bob: "I'm Tom."

I stood in the bar, my heart in my throat, thoroughly awed that I should meet him again after eleven years. Tom Marino was a legend of San Francisco heartbreak with Steve and me. Steve had a torrid affair with him, I had a childish crush on him based on the times I went out with the two of them, and everything Steve repeated to me, including of course every detail of their very inventive, reciprocal, hot sex. "A blond Sicilian," Steve would say, as if that said it all, pursing his lips and sucking air like he'd just tasted something very hot, or was about to say something in French. I remember a very compelling story about Steve getting up between bouts to piss and Tom coming up behind him and fucking him in the ass while he pissed, standing over the toilet.

After the gay parade in June of '78, drunk and stoned on MDA, we found our way to the 'N Touch. Steve and Tom had had some sort of spat and were hanging out at opposite ends of the bar, and I found myself standing behind Tom with my arms around his waist and my hand down the overalls he wore with no shirt, slowly stroking his straight-up cock while Steve glared at us. ("You go ahead and screw him if you want to; it's him I'll never speak to again if you do," he'd growled.) A week later, when they'd all but stopped seeing each other, Tom called up unexpectedly to tell Steve he'd taken a job in Texas and was leaving town immediately. It was a Saturday evening; Steve and I stopped by Tom's place on our way to Polk Street. When we went up, we found the apartment stripped of furniture, boxes piled around, Tom on the phone confirming his flight. He and Steve talked a while quietly while I waited in the bare kitchen, coming on to the MDA we'd taken before leaving Steve's and feeling very tragic. And then we left, Tom saying, "Keep in touch," though it was clear nobody would. On the street, there were balloons and streamers and empty beer bottles rolling into the gutter and street vendors taking down their booths—the tail end of a street fair, when Polk looks cheesier than ever. It was the picture of abandonment, and

Steve and I both started to cry, and then laughed ruefully at each other for being such saps. "I can't believe that fucker did this to me!" Steve kept saying—meaning, made him love someone at a time when he was being deliberately promiscuous and getting serious with no one.

When I returned with the drinks he was talking to Bob. He turned to me: "Don't I know you from somewhere?" I told my little tale ("Picture this: Sicily, 1922..."), complete with the dick-holding episode. He beamed and nodded his head, but I couldn't judge his reactions in terms of me, now. He went back to his book after nervously prattling on about his whereabouts for the intervening years; I picked up the dice and shook them.

When Bob and I got up the next morning, he'd put a note under the door before leaving, with his address and phone number in the city—"It was nice to see you again." Bob: "If you don't see that means he's interested, you're crazy."

October 14, 1989

Up early on a Saturday morning—Richard slept over, got up and walked Henry, and left for work. He's an acquaintance of Bob's who started playing racquetball with us in August. I thought he was very cute and sweet, and developed a crush on him that I'd assumed would remain fanciful, as Bob said Richard lived with someone. We undressed beside each other at the Y, played racquetball, showered—I felt constrained not to look too directly at him naked, not wanting to seem like some kind of lech. At dinners afterward, I found him smart, fun, and endearing. He's eight years older than me, from Kentucky, co-owns a dusty old metaphysical bookstore on Polk Street with a ninety-something-year-old Gurdjieffian lady who resembles a creature out of Tolkein. (The narrow shop always smells of incense and pizza from Victor's next door. I'd avoided it all my years on Polk Street because of the window full of Gurdjieff books, each picturing the guru's seal-like, mustachioed face.) He's got longish blond hair, glasses, dresses mainly in dapper khakis and white shirts; he's a few inches shorter than me, has a nice trim body and a compact little butt (this much I noted at the Y). He let it be known that he and the fellow he lives with are business partners and roommates, but no longer lovers. (*Danger, Will Robinson!*) Like me, he's HIV+ but asymptomatic.

Three weeks ago, still on vacation from my editorial labors at Riddley House, I met Bob and Richard for racquetball and dinner. At Zuni, Richard sat with his leg pressed against mine under the table while I laughed about the flurry of creepy obscene voicemails I've gotten since leaving my phone number on Tom Marino's machine. So much for Kismet.

Bob wanted to see a photo show hanging at the Brig, so we drove there for a drink and found it jammed for the crux of Leather Week (that's Richard's and my cute-meet now: we fell in love during Leather Week). Shoved together, jostled, and yelling in each other's ears, we covered several key points: both lonely, weary of trying to meet someone but badly wanting to.

Bob, our inadvertent matchmaker ("I invited him to play because *I* wanted to see him in the shower!" he complained, but not very seriously), now asked to be dropped off at his car first and wondered if Richard would mind driving me home? I was beginning to feel a bit anxious, but also excited. It was easy enough to say, "Want to come in and meet my dog?" We sat on the couch talking for an hour. Although by this time I felt fairly sure of him, I was loath to make the first physical move in case I was somehow completely deluded. Then he put his hand on my leg and leaned over to kiss me very tenderly. This was my first romantic kiss since Jack—a long time. "Thank you," I said, and meant it.

The sex was very emotional (and his first since getting sober a few years ago, he told me later). We both felt so deprived and shell-shocked, the slightest act was thrilling. When we stripped off our clothes and sat back a moment looking at each other, cocks hard and dripping, he took off his glasses and set them on the desk, said, "I'm going to eat you alive," and dove at me.

December 3, 1989
Senior Editorial Assistant to the Stars—that's me, as of last

week. This manuscript, the spiritual autobiography of "Gwen Arden," a retired movie star of the fifties, got dropped on my desk at Riddley House some months back, one of my eccentric boss's cocktail party acquisitions. Many rewrites later, I'd sent it out for jacket comment to the author's eye-popping list of celebrity pals. (It's interesting to note that Bob Hope lives on Bob Hope Drive, which must make it simple with cabs.) It started on Monday, when Roddy McDowell called me. Then I came back from lunch and listened to a voicemail I almost shrugged off as a prank—from Katharine Hepburn. ("Where aaarrre you anyway, out eeeaaattting, I suppose?") She called back later and it was so surreal I might as well have been chatting with Rocky Squirrel. The next day, Patricia Neal called up, a bit breathless: "I hope I'm not too late, I've just come back from Africa, where I saw *all* the animals!" I pictured her like Noah, with exotics marching by in twos. She was so nice, I guess I can't go on doing my impression of her Maxwell House commercial. ("Moooy hwoosband's a wrrriiiiittter...") Van Johnson was a letdown; he mailed in his comments, written on the back of my letter in what appeared to be lipstick.

Of course once I'd bragged to everyone and played back my voicemail on speaker phone so many times the publisher came out of his glass office and frowned, I got a deluge of crank responses from the likes of Frank Sinatra and Mr. Ed.

December 29, 1989

Dinner last night at Anchor Oyster Bar on Castro; Richard making an oyster's lips speak with a toothpick—"Hi, Kevvie!"—causing the waiter, who resembles a young Paul Simon, to giggle.

Later, lying together in my bed panting, cum drying on our chests, I felt a rush of tenderness. What exactly we do at this point to reach orgasm, so different from what we might once have done, hardly matters: I love him, I could be excited just jacking off and nuzzling his face.

1991

October 26, 1991

An hour ago, Richard said, regarding the approach of Halloween, "Every holiday since I started AZT, I think, well, this's my last Easter, Christmas, whatever. I thought that first Christmas we were together"—'89, when he was dangerously anemic—"would be my last."

Caught a glimpse, in the bathroom at Richard's place last night, of the back of my head in a shaving mirror, and thought something had gotten splashed on me. I've suddenly got a spattering of gray hair, after never having any. Richard said solemnly, "I've turned your hair gray."

Seeing Dr. J. once a week for the last several months. Some tears, more the kind that spring out during vehement recounting and are angrily dashed away than the flat-out boo-hoo sort I'd think a waste of time. I told him about the breezy card from my mother, mailed to work as she no longer has my address, which made no mention of Richard or his health.

Dr. J. widens his scared-horse eyes. "I'm hearing a lot of anger." You bet I'm angry. My lover's having the life slowly drained out of him, I can probably look forward to the same, and we can't change anything significant in our living situation—

he goes on sharing a household with Ron and spending nights with me in the apartment I now rent in their other building around the block—because he doesn't think he has a future. I think maybe I've been off my head for the last five years—since Jack's diagnosis. How else could I continue to do the mundane day-to-day things, work productively, enjoy anything, laugh—but by becoming insane enough to live with something so unacceptable?

1992

June 8, 1992 (Santa Fe)

The little phone in the kitchen of our casita trilled at 8:35 this morning, waking us both from sound sleep. Richard got it: Gwen Arden calling. "If you go to a bookstore today, see if there's one on daily life in the pueblo, would you?" I'd been having the rare enough sexual dream, watching, up-close, a muscular ass flexing in and out over another—then, the sensation of being fucked by the Dick of Life. I was watching it as if on a screen, then I was feeling it: not hard to understand, knowing how much the visual has to suffice for me right now.

Yesterday, Sunday, Gwen came to pick us up at 10:30 to take us to lunch at Bishop's Lodge, her usual rich-people type place, but very beautiful surroundings and a lavish buffet. I couldn't think of much to say, but Gwen and Richard talked quite a lot about their cats. She did regale us with some Hollywood gossip about Jennifer Jones ("the most insecure woman I ever met") who had to have a hairdresser and make-up man do her before she'd put her head out her front door. And on the recently written-up liaison between Danny Kaye and Laurence Olivier: "Of course everyone *knew* about it—they just didn't put it on the news. Like Jack Kennedy and Angie

Dickinson. He flew her to India on Air Force One, right after
Jackie made the same trip." In the middle of telling this, Gwen
said, "Excuse me, I *have* to do this—" and held a napkin over
her face just below her eyes, like a harem girl. I thought for a
moment she was taking out a contact, or using nasal spray—but
in a flash she'd passed a bread plate behind the napkin, and it
reappeared with a ball of chewed-up food (gristle or fish bone,
I presume), which she quickly obscured with a cracker.

Afterward, she drove us by a celebrated woodcarver's
shop, where she insisted that we each pick one object of Mr.
Ortega's, her treat. St. Francis statues made partly of driftwood were his specialty, seconded by birds and angels (with
driftwood for the pleated robes). I picked up a small angel—I
liked the elaborately carved wings. Richard chose a stick with
three fat birds on it. Gwen tossed in a phallus-headed St.
Francis and wrote out a $200 check to Mrs. Ortega. "You
really have an eye for what's good," Gwen told me. "You
picked the best angel out right away, that's very good."

"*Why not vicuna, if the lady's paying,*" I said. "Only last
week I picked two pairs of shoes at Nordstrom, when Richard
was buying."

June 9, 1992
Just back from morning and lunch with Gwen. She picked us
up armed with several pink plastic grocery bags and an old

tablespoon, and we drove to the Santuario de Chimayó, where Richard was to get some blessed miracle dirt to rub on his face later (for the unpleasant, itchy molluscum eruptions). We passed through a beautiful panorama of juniper-dotted reddish hills and dramatic billows of white clouds on the drive there. We reached the pretty old adobe church, with its ancient wooden doors. It was dim and stuffy inside, with a mix of tourists and faithful who, presumably, had walked or crawled all the way from somewhere for a better shot at a miracle.

We stepped down to a squat doorway at the back of the church (I idly noted the sign reading "watch your head" and bashed mine) and into a small grotto full of Jesus, Mary, and St. Francis dolls, one wall lined with painted icons, nasty modern 3-D Jesus/Baby Jesus/Jesus pictures, yellowed and curling graduation photos of dead people, and other tawdry poverty-Catholic stuff—then a wall opposite filled with crutches, leg braces, and suchlike, left behind by those miraculously cured of what brought them there—it looked like the rough draft of a Plath poem. In an even smaller adjoining grotto you had to crouch further to enter, there was a pile of dirt spilling out of a gash in the wood floor that'd been taken from somewhere or other sacred and double-blessed by priests. Richard got down to scoop some up amid the flickering bleeding-Jesus votive holders, and I felt a need to sneeze violently (and no wonder; everything looked like it could use a good vacuuming), coupled with an urge to laugh that drove me back out into the first grotto to stare at a dirty doll-baby wearing a tiara and housed in a sort of glass coffin.

Outside, Gwen allowed me to take her picture with Richard (at a specified great distance) in front of the sagging, buttery-looking sanctuary gates, then we drove off to the Inn at Chimayó for lunch on a catalpa shaded terrace, surrounded by giant salmon-colored poppies. We talked about health, illness, death (assisted), and living in the present—and the strangeness (to me) of living with your past self in constant attendance on the Movie Channel. I told Gwen about Vonnegut's Billy Pilgrim and the idea of being "unstuck in time." "Interesting," she said, summoning a waiter for more iced tea and changing the subject back to cats.

1993

January 3, 1993

Here's that time when Richard would sleep on while I got up to walk Henry ("There's money in my pants pocket," he'd invariably mutter before drifting off again). When we returned with muffins or sweet rolls, Henry racing up and down the apartment in his joy at returning to find Richard here, he'd have his head buried in the covers so Henry couldn't lick his face.

On Friday, New Year's Day, I went around the corner to Ron's to pick up the ceramic dachshund he'd found in the bottom of one of Richard's drawers, presumably something he'd squirreled away to give me at Christmas. The ashes had been brought home, in a brown paper-wrapped container. Ron asked if I wanted to hold them. They were oddly heavy, and I handed them back pretty quickly. I tried not to look beyond Richard's desk to his little mouse-hole of a bedroom, with all his clothes thrown about as he'd left them, and the unmade bed.

February 26, 1993

Went with Bob on Tuesday night to see ACT's notorious gangster-noir "Duchess of Malfi." Watched with pounding heart the scene where she's shown the wax effigies of her dead children and husband. "Persuade a wretch that's broke upon the wheel/to have all his bones new set; entreat him live/To be executed again." *That's pretty realistic*, I thought.

Dreamt one night this week I was weeping over Richard, who lay, still alive, in a hospital bed, his face turned away. "Don't die, don't leave me, I don't want to live without you," I said, the usual. He turned to look at me and I felt terribly awkward and taken aback: it was Jack, not Richard.

I went alone to see *Howard's End* on Friday night—then took the underground to Castro, plunging from Edwardian London into the pitch-black, smoky, and deafening interior of the Detour. I've been out of that so long now the people around me looked like extras hired to portray a gay bar crowd in a heavy-handed movie like *Cruising*. Wake up, Rip: tricking was no breeze eight years ago when I met Jack and happily bailed out—it's no easier now.

April 7, 1993

Last Thursday night I went out after work with Jane and Carol from Riddley House—and Jane's old friend Matt Galante, of whom she's always speaking—and he was smart and friendly and attractive, a tanned, dark-skinned, slender Italian—and the word came back by the next morning that he'd be interested in hearing from me.

Two nights ago, he came over for our much-anticipated

date. We sat on the couch and talked over a glass of wine, did not leap upon each other at once, which would've made things much easier. In spite of our both having expressed interest in "going out" after Thursday's meeting, nothing was quickly assumed. We talked through my making dinner and eating it by candlelight while Henry scurried around under the table.

We took our glasses into the living room after, pulled out books, and lay about on the rug with exaggerated ease, but with occasional heavy pauses in the conversation. I saw I was expected to make the first physical sign if anything was to happen. He got up and said half-heartedly he ought to be going. I stood in front of him, close, and said that sitting on his futon last week watching movies with Jane and Carol I'd felt very attracted to him, and still felt so; began to put my arms around him. "Let's sit down a minute," he said. He too was attracted, he said, but was concerned sex not throw a wrench into our getting to be friends (as best I understood him; essentially, he wanted some pursuit, I think). Going slowly was fine with me, I said. "Do you mind if I kiss you?" He was amenable. This kiss was very wonderful and awkward as such moments always are with someone brand new—heads, lips colliding. We embraced, and I inhaled the human boy scent of his hair, his shirt (cigarette smoke), his cheek. We kissed some more, stopping to look at each other a minute—*who are you, anyway?*—kissed again, fitting our mouths more smoothly. From here it was only a matter of stages. Could we lie back a bit (and grind our bursting crotches against each other)? Could we pull off our T-shirts so we could feel a bit of flesh against flesh?

"I don't think we should have sex on our first date," he said, without much conviction. "It's good sometimes to have blue balls."

"Then let's just neck some more," I said. It wasn't comfortable on the couch: one of us was always squashed or slipping off. We moved to the bed, taking off our shoes. I let my hand start rubbing his erection through his jeans and he did the same to me. He decided to get undressed, then walked naked into the kitchen and smoked a cigarette leaning out the window in the dark. We rehearsed our respective ideas of safe sex, our current handicaps (I had a scraped spot on my dick from a fevered wank on Saturday sans lube; he *might* have some lingering anal warts). These clinical revelations failed to quash our ardor, and we resumed in earnest. He has a very nice, slender brown body, a heavy patch of black hair from his flat stomach down, a cock that points straight up his stomach at twelve o'clock. We kissed, rubbed, and wanked each other with insufficient lube (I'd thought it bad luck to prepare too much).

April 9, 1993

I went over to Matt's last evening bearing flowers (snapdragons and irises) and a pocketful of ribbed condoms from Condomania on Castro Street. We started kissing at the door (he removed my glasses and placed them carefully on a shelf), pulled off our clothes very soon (he has a fetching way of shrugging out of his baggy shorts and over-sized T-shirt) and lay on the futon couch. This was much better than our nervous and tipsy first night; we seemed of one mind—we'd thought about it since and had gotten very horny. He has a thickish, tapered dick that stays very hard, even when he seems heavy-lidded and lackadaisical. We decided the scrape on my cock was OK now, and he sucked me; the sensation was fantastic. Going without for so long has heightened my sensitivity. It's an almost shocking realization that I'm at it with someone five years younger, and as horny, even hornier than me. I asked if I could fuck him. He'd be quite willing, he said, but didn't feel capable at the moment; would I like to get fucked? A bit more of his jerking and sucking on my dick, while I stroked his straight-up cock, and I decided to try it. I rolled a ribbed rubber onto him (no loss of erection, hooray!), slapped a blob of lube on my nervous butt, and began trying to get it in. Barring the occasional lone sex-toy play, a very different kind of thing, I've not done this since the first months with Jack—nearly seven years ago. You don't forget what's necessary. It began to work, but I was so tight, I felt absolutely skewered. He began giving some dramatic thrusts as I hovered astride him, jacking off. The feeling of giving something up to the other person, of making yourself vulnerable, of being totally changed, made *other* by the thing you're doing—it's a transcendent experience. (I can hear Gary Reed saying something terribly rude about now.)

We ate dinner. I felt awkward again, dressed and chatting, trying to get a fix on this attractive, intelligent stranger. Can I trust him? Will he crush me down the road a ways?

After washing up we sat back on the couch talking, then making out again. We kissed slowly, luxuriously; I reached down and felt his dick poking up in his shorts, and ground mine against him. It was exhausted, preoccupied necking, no longer racing to an orgasm, but rising to a certain pitch, pausing, starting up again, like eating something delicious slowly. I left at midnight with my lips sore and my head spinning. This is good medicine.

April 16, 1993

We've spent a few nights away from each other. Matt mentioned the other evening he had plans for the next night. He didn't say, but I assumed he was seeing Will, the hairdresser he was "tapering off" dating before meeting me. ("I've already made him cry once," Matt noted sadly.) I went out for dinner and some drinks with Nate that night and then walked up Castro to wait for a bus home, whipped by the suddenly chilly wind. At some point in the half-hour wait before I gave up and walked home, I felt a sort of psychic tap on the shoulder and turned back toward the sidewalk in time to see Matt and a stoop-shouldered blond in a black leather jacket disappearing around the corner. I had a touching stab of familiarity at the sight of Matt's unruly dark hair and dorky black-framed glasses, followed by queasy feelings of distrust. I stood there catching cold in the bitter wind, thinking of the love that had been a given with Richard almost from the first moment—how happy the most domestic evening with him seemed, cast against the cold doubleness of someone younger, cautious, and new.

April 19, 1993

Yesterday, after a late lunch at The Brick Hut in Berkeley with Jane and her girlfriend and sunbathing in some park, we were dropped off back at Matt's studio. He shrugged out of his clothes and lay back on the couch offering himself. We were both very into sucking each other's dicks. After much approaching and backing away from orgasm, Matt decided I could fuck him. I rolled on a rubber and slicked his asshole with lube. We were lying on our sides; he reached back to guide my hard-on in; "Hold on a minute; OK, go ahead…" and I slid inside his tight, warm hole. He stays hard while getting fucked; I reached around to jack him off but he put a hand down to stop me: "Careful, you'll make me come." At first I moved slowly—then, "You can be a little rougher if you want," he said, and I started really plowing in and out, turning his head to the side to shove my tongue in his mouth, and reaching back down to jack his dick. This went on for a timeless stretch—till, wet and panting, we came at the same time. He had a cigarette going so fast I didn't even see him light it; maybe it had been waiting in the ashtray. We lay in each other's arms talking and listening to old, scratchy Janis Ian records. I walked home in the fog at eleven, freezing in my now-insufficient shorts and a borrowed sweater, lips raw, dick still half-hard and dripping, sated and happy.

April 26, 1993

Things are either slacking off, or normalizing, with Matt. Last weekend we were together on Saturday and Sunday, then I made dinner for us here on Tuesday. That was the occasion that threw me into doubt, because between him being tired, Henry persistently leaping onto the bed and having to be pushed off, and a timetable being imposed—dinner in the oven—sex was a bit forced and less dramatically good than previously. No big deal, except that he'd made it so clear that "people should stop having sex the moment it becomes like blowing your nose!" and I thought, *Oh no, here he is reaching for a hanky.*

Thursday night we went with Bob to see *The Night Larry Kramer Kissed Me* at Fort Mason, and Matt was affectionate, reaching to hold my hand during the show. But he had to go straight home in order to rise for a work meeting at six, so he didn't come along to dinner with us. "Our first date without sex!" he said brightly, as if this were an important milestone. *May they be few*, I thought.

Friday night he was busy with depressed lesbian friend Carol Ann (who comes up so often in this way I suspect her of being a sort of Bunbury) and when I called from work just to say I knew he was busy but I wanted to see him and was looking forward to Saturday, he said, unkindly, "If you're horny, you should go out and have sex with someone else. That's what I'd do."

May 3, 1993
Friday I went to Matt's shortly after work; it smelled of cooking outside his studio door when I arrived—he was pressure-cooking black beans for bean dip to take to a housewarming later. We fell on each other soon after I'd walked in: he sucked me off till I yanked away and shot; I put a rubber on his hard dick and got astride it, and came again that way. I was, as always with him, extremely excited, can't kiss enough; it's a kind of consuming of each other.

He was affectionate at the party, staying close to me all evening. When we left at 1:30, we walked to an all-night restaurant and got sandwiches and more wine, and dove without preamble into the only real serious discussion we've had about what's going on with us after a month: his experience of losing his independence and identity in a four-year relationship that began in college; my plea that he not deliberately stifle any feeling between us just because of that. "I know sometimes I'm very cold to you," he said. After announcing that this might be a good time to try having me sleep over, by the time we left he'd changed his mind, and we kissed good-bye at 2:30 on the deserted corner of Sanchez and Market.

He called up at noon the next day, Saturday, and I walked over in bright hot sun, to read and sunbathe together in the Gay Belt up at the top of Dolores Park with a hundred other gay men. Matt just stripped to some bikini underwear sitting on his towel: "They all just *hate* it—they just buzz when I do this." Speedos are de rigour; I wore my favorite worn blue gym shorts, so we were both out of fashion. Next he wanted to go to Midnight Sun to watch the video they were supposed to be showing of the recent Washington March. I'd hoped to take our sweaty bodies back to his place and fuck. "We've already had sex in the last twenty-four hours so I don't feel sexual," he said. Our sojourn in the Midnight Sun proved brief: a young queen standing at the bar was shouting down the speeches—"Where's the music?"—and pretty shortly music was duly reinstated; Matt was indignant.

After some errands we strolled back to Matt's place. Surprise! He felt sexual after all. We had a very hot encounter begun in the tiny kitchen, Matt sitting in a chair with his legs spread in loose baggy shorts. I crouched and pulled the swelling head of his dick out from under the hem of his shorts, and sucked it. He yanked my shorts down and off, and I stood, sunburned and tingling, with my cock sticking out hard, in just socks and hightops, while he blew me and reached up to twist my nipples. After, he suggested we try napping together a short while, and, to my delight, as the sun slanted over us from the one dusty little window, we drifted off spoon-situated on the futon couch, and both slept for twenty minutes or so. This was our first extended, naked, post-sex lie-down together, and it felt very nice. I felt a taste of that sweetness one wants so, and mostly does without.

June 1, 1993
Matt calls, back from the weekend at Russian River with his ex-boyfriend: "Hi, sweetheart, I'm back and I'm horny! I didn't have sex with anyone while I was up there, you know." I mentioned his coldness at our last meeting, and he spluttered, feigning shock: "I'm not prepared to mount a defense, by phone."

"Thanks for telling me that," I said, meaning, that he hadn't screwed around over the weekend, "instead of just letting me wonder."

"I shouldn't have told you. What if I *had* had sex with someone, then?"

I walked over to his place in the early evening. He answered the door sleepy-eyed, hot and damp like a napping baby. I listened to him chatter about his camp-out, then we began to kiss, and had the sort of grateful, reverential sex one does after five days without. I was holding, squeezing, prodding his warm ass a lot; we'd only just gotten our clothes pulled off and gone back to kissing, dick thrusting against dick, when he said, "Wanna try it?" and reached for a party-red rubber. This, on a muggy summer evening, with late sun and sounds of a backyard handyman's sawing and whistling drifting in at the window, was an unexpected pleasure. He lay on his stomach, and as I began to ease my dick in, I reached under him with a wet hand to slick up the hot head of his dick. I was pulling his head around to kiss him when his tightly clenched ass gave way and my cock slid up and in. He was moaning quietly; I fucked steadily, both hands gripping his ass, pulling the cheeks apart, squeezing them tightly together on my dick. I went back to jacking him, and his cum squirted between my fingers as I gripped the swollen head of his dick with the ring of my thumb and forefinger, and I came with my hips smacking wetly against his butt.

July 3, 1993

A week ago Friday I left work early and bussed over in 90 degree heat to meet Matt at the Castro for film festival *Boys Don't Cry 2* shorts. He'd been watching movies all afternoon, and promptly announced he was too hot to stay any longer, and I was left alone, a good thing as it turned out, since the last short, *Deaf Heaven*, was a beautiful but grueling AIDS story about a guy swimming and sitting in the sauna at a gym with elderly Jewish men between visits to his dying lover in the hospital. The theatre was stifling and the packed crowd almost silent but for an occasional sniffle, until, at a very painful moment in the film, an almost inaudible sound escaped someone not far from me, and the entire row shook with sobs.

I walked out into the bright late afternoon sunshine wiping my eyes, and walked three blocks over to Matt's and into a different world. He was lying naked with an electric fan trained on him, drinking a margarita. After I attempted to blow him to orgasm ("I'm too hot to come, but you can try"), enjoying a good wank in the attempt, we lay about naked and sipping our icy drinks, listening to novelty records like Mrs. Miller, Mia Farrow humming the cracked lullaby from *Rosemary's Baby*, and Mary Ann Mobley's "Get Yourself a College Girl." We walked out for pizza, tipsy, at about nine, amid the parade weekend crush on Castro Street, and kissed good-bye afterward on the street.

July 5, 1993
Just spent a long day with Matt. He'd asked if I'd help him take down his stereo and pull out all the rat's nest of wires to try and figure out why the speakers are crackling or dead half the time. Soon after I arrived at 11:30, we began hauling his videos and tapes out from the shelves holding the stereo components,

exposing an amazing amount of dust, dirt, change, phone numbers and names on scraps of paper and matchbooks, political buttons, and condom packets (mostly long out of date). Both large speakers proved to have been partially disconnected, probably gnawed by the cat. It took several hours to take everything out, clean, re-wire, and replace. Finished, we lay on the couch drinking lemonade, and began making out. He was horny (all those old phone numbers?) and we got very excited just kissing. Ever since the weekend in Forestville, when our lovemaking was particularly frantic and nasty, sex has been ratcheted up a notch.

I've fucked him the last couple of times; today, he seemed to be moving toward the opposite, and I suddenly very much felt like it. This was really the first time I've relaxed into it properly, never felt put off by discomfort; took it on my back, down and dirty. We were kissing sloppily and my lip bashed his front tooth, leaving a blood-bruise. I was jacking off, and when I came the jets hit my chin as he pulled out and slammed back in in rhythm to my spurting. He'd gotten his hair cut short after our trip, for the first time since I've known him, and he looks very cute and boyish. I've been feeling a bit romantic on and off as a result, though I'd come back from the trip determined to match his detachment out of bed.

July 13, 1993
Phone conversation with Matt last night; he likes these long,

teenage-girl gab fests, from work gossip to the weird. Long discussion about how penis and penis-size oriented I am, according to him, whereas he, Matt, doesn't really think about them that much, doesn't care if they're large, or even hard. If I'd read more feminism, I wouldn't set so much store by dick. Somebody's been at his French deconstructionist feminism again. This is so at odds with the ever-smuttier sex we've been having, I find it somehow endearingly crackpot.

He went to the doctor, a thing he mostly avoids, and had left me a voicemail at work earlier in the day with a full report: "The doctor felt my wiener and stuck his finger up my butt. I've got to poo in several containers. I have a referral to have my anal warts looked at, and I took an HIV test." This is all an about-face from his previous head-in-the-sand stance. I wasn't prepared for what came next. "When you realize somebody cares about you, you start to care more about taking care of yourself. And I realize you do care about me, and that's caused a sort of change in me, I guess." (How many times in the last week has he reminded me he isn't looking for a boyfriend?) On the phone I asked if, when the doctor pulled his finger out of Matt's butt, he looked at it and burst into Merman-esque "You're not sick, you're *just in love!*" I begin to think I may hear it from him yet.

August 8, 1993
I brought groceries over to Matt's to make dinner on Friday

night. He was tired and napping when I came to the door, and in a gentle, non-combative mood. We kissed, and the groceries sat bagged on the kitchen table while I hauled my dick out without taking my pants off and he sucked the engorged head noisily, a focus that almost always makes me ready to shoot in a hurry. After staggering to the couch for more sucking, I had my pants shoved down enough to turn on my side and rub his dick against my sweat-damp asshole—and it began to feel real good. I jumped up, got lube and a rubber, rolled it onto his jutting dick, and ended up squatting over his lap and jacking his dick with my asshole while he jacked away at mine, and I shot over his shoulder and down his chest. He pulled out, stripped off the rubber and masturbated with my cum while I sucked his balls, kissed him, and finally, bit his nipples, which, as always, did the trick.

Later, I pulled out the copy of *Saul's Book* I'd picked up for him, and read him the pool hall passage I've masturbated over untold times. But his feminist sensiblities were back in place and he turned up his nose: "I don't like pornography."

August 30, 1993

Friday was a hot, jumbled-up moving day at Riddley House—half the office being moved from one end to the other, and that doom feeling that some folks aren't going to be unpacking their boxes. (The last five years have been like *The Pit and the*

Pendulum—once a year the reorganization blade swings.)

I walked to Matt's in the early evening, fell into sex almost before speaking, culminating with my fucking him bent over the couch. We ate quickly after, and headed out in the warm night to a building on upper Market and the *Dark Shadows* party. (Matt had hooked up through an ad with other aficionados of the old horror soap I used to watch when I came in from school in the sixth grade.) The party consisted of about a dozen very homely and socially crippled individuals sitting around a '70s-style apartment watching *DS* videos, looking at a photo album of the host's recent trip to a convention, and listening to lots of little *DS* trivia bits from a bulgy character with geeky glasses and an oily blond ponytail who was missing some of his tongue and wasn't easy to understand. This old circa '67-'71 soap opera is being issued on video; the partygoers excitedly compared their purchasing sprees: "*I'm* already on number 178!"

"That's a lie! Number 178 won't be released till next week!"

"I've spent more on *DS* videos than I did on my car!"

"Did you know Joe Morse's character changed actors after episode 63? He was fired for alcoholism and replaced with Jeff Sweeny!"

"Let's run that blooper tape again."

The blooper tape was an endless compilation of quick moments where booms swung into camera range, tombstones fell over, characters flubbed their lines ("Angelique is a witch and she must *fry*! Er, *die*!"), and best, flies landed on actors' noses, which seemed to have happened a lot. I managed to knock over a big glass of water (forget a drink with this crowd) on the carpet, perilously near someone's script autographed by Grayson Hall, which was dramatically snatched up and examined for damage.

September 3, 1993

Early morning: walking Henry up and down Pearl Street just now, it was foggy and slightly misting, and I remembered for just a second the way the air felt to me in those first unreal, excited, and terrified days when I arrived sixteen years ago. The combination of cool, wet air, and the mildewy smell of decaying wooden houses, the exhalations of old rooms—I'd never seen Victorians before, so the Castro seemed like a movie back lot—brings back that overwhelming illusion that a man with beautiful eyes and terrific lust is coming toward me, is just around the corner.

Matt says he's terribly depressed, "the worst in five years," and you can tell: his answering machine message has changed from Susan Hayward bellowing "Broadway doesn't go for booze and dope!" to Anne Sexton intoning *Macbeth*, "All my pretty ones? Did you say all?" It's hard not to expect I'll turn out to be the culprit, though he claims, asked outright, that's not it. My timid suggestion that being alive and relatively healthy, given what's happening all around us (his latest test came back negative), ought to be purely reason for joy, met with annoyance. "You've developed this cheery little philosophy over the past few years that being suicidal in a world where others are dying of AIDS is just self-indulgent. Well that may work for you, but it doesn't for me."

October 12, 1993

Post-breakup letter from Matt arrives. Some deposition-like salvos: "I would like, at this point, to state that I did call you on Saturday, *but you never returned my call*;" some grudging flattery: "I won't easily find another as intelligent, handsome, a good lay...." It was computer-printed, with a handwritten P.S., enclosing a Guatamalan prayer bracelet, which apparently works like a wishbone—"I've put one on, wishing we'll be together talking and laughing again, as we once were."

Buddy called last night from New York. We talked a long time, me catching him up on Matt, work, my writing; heard his news: he's left Ed, is now in love with a forty-eight-year-old man. "That's what I want," I said. "A nice mature guy. *I* want to be the young one!"

"Well honey, you can, it's easy!" Buddy said.

1994

January 19, 1994

Today is my thirty-eighth birthday. I got a call from Dr. B. at the Health Department last week: "How'd you like an all-expenses paid trip to Bethesda Naval Hospital in Washington, D.C.? Tony Fauci really wants to get a lymph node from you!"

Read Susan Bergman's *Anonymity* (not very good, and not very subtly homophobic) and then a bound galley of Herve Guibert's *The Compassion Protocol*, a diary-like narrative of his brief upswing on an early release of DDI—wow. I've since found his earlier *To the Friend Who Did Not Save My Life* and devoured it.

February 27, 1994

Tuesday was Richard's birthday, so I was thinking about him. I ended up leaving work at noon, taking a cab with Louise to the Randy Shilts memorial service at Glide Church. There were lots of police because of expected picketing from the abominable "Reverend" Phelps, and a huge crowd of gays and friends filled the street in front of the church, which was already packed. The speeches were broadcast out into the street: Marcus Conant, Michael Denneny, Roy Aarons. When we first walked into the crowd, the choir was belting out the same song a smaller group of them had sung at Richard's memorial, the one I'd thought was saying "best, best," but was really saying "blessed."

As I stood rocking back on my heels in the crowd, Rev. Cecil delivering his brief, rousing eulogy, I let myself substitute Richard for Randy now and then in what he was saying. And when I squinted, my eyes full of tears, up toward the top of the church, I could easily imagine Richard standing up there, casually balancing on a parapet, like George Kirby in *Topper*.

March 29, 1994

Friday Edward called me into his office (the ominous "Got a moment?") and, to my amazement, informed me I was being promoted to associate editor, and would be moving into an office. And a pleasing salary leap.

I went straight from work to celebrate, meeting Gina at the Giraffe, and going on with her to dinner. Later, I called Bob, who was working late at the shop, and talked him into going out for a beer. He picked me up at 10:30 and we drank and talked through a couple of Folsom bars. A guy Bob knows from the Magazine came up and stuck with us at the last bar— energetic, aggressive, slightly scary. He turned out to be Scott Taylor, a former porn star and Nob Hill Theater performer. He seemed to be very interested in me; it also seemed clear he was a sort of hand-to-mouth type like Michael Harper—if he came home with you, it might be because he had nowhere else to go. He kept referring to his most famous film—*Rough Magic* or *Stick Shift*, I don't remember. Turns out he's well known for his self-suck capabilities. "You're very attractive," he said, standing closer, when Bob went to buy beers. I shrugged it off; but it was nice to be flirted with.

May 5, 1994
Art opening and book party for one of my authors last evening. Went in a cab in misting rain to the gallery, which I'd been telling people sounded from the address like it must be somewhere near where the old VD clinic used to be. Actually, it *is* the old VD clinic: up the stairs and exactly in the same (gutted) space, with the same view I used to turn my head toward while my blood was drawn for STD check-ups and later, the Hepatitis-B study.

The previous day at work, the last hour was spent in a mandatory gathering listening to happy propaganda: Celebrate Our Success! Accounting department drones were cheered for staying late to xerox the budget, the publisher's assistant cheered for "taking such good care of him." I thought I might die like a rock star, choking on my vomit.

May 29, 1994
Called Gina to maybe have dinner, but she was busy bathing

her gaga Mom and couldn't come out, so I got take-out and a porno tape.

Somebody of interest caught my eye at Muscle Sisters today: short blond hair, slightly pitted, interesting face, both humorous and nasty looking, nicely built, but not exceptionally muscular; in my class, I almost thought. We happened to shower beside each other and I sneaked a look at his nice butt and short, thickish dick. His hair was cut close to his head, kinky, with sixties sideburns. Then, there he was in the mirror right around the other side of the bank of lockers as I dressed and I couldn't help looking, though he obviously could look back in the mirror and see me doing so. His dick swelled and began to rise as he toweled off, aware of my attention. He pulled on some baggy, elastic-waisted shorts without putting on any underwear, flipping his punky dick inside right at the last, leaving me with a pretty image to ponder. When I emerged on Hayes Street he was standing against the building, one leg cocked up on the brick wall, staring straight ahead through wraparound dark glasses. I paused a moment to notice him, half-thinking he'd grab at his awfully-accessible cock and turn to look at me, but he didn't, so I had to assume he was waiting for someone else. I couldn't have approached him cold for the world.

June 19, 1994
Gay Pride Day. Thinking of '82's Tony Salerno—my Summer

of Love, though I didn't know it. How the HIV must've been flying between Gary and Michael, me, Tony, and all the one-nighters. (June '82 being the time the Clinic Study thinks I sero-converted—an odd term, that sounds like coming around to a certain way of thinking.)

Strange, reading my account from that June of being heavily cruised at the Detour and having to turn suitors away to get to Tony. Have I altered so much? (Arno: *Have I changed much then?*) Or is it what I've gone through that's marked me? The city's packed with cute guys for this weekend, and I know I'd just be invisible if I went out and tried to wedge my way into the jammed bars. Bob said at dinner last night, of going through throngs of young, hunky gay men to pick up a book at A Different Light the night before, "It's all cute guys in gangs of six friends—and for me, there's just you."

July 16, 1994

I went to meet Gina for dinner at The Metro on Sunday evening, and sipped a Margarita in a very lively crowd for half an hour awaiting her. I became interested in a handsome, though acne-scarred, man in a tight baseball outfit who'd given me an initial long, searching appraisal when I first sat down. After much looking, and then discussion of him with Gina when she'd arrived in a cloud of pot smoke, I noticed his wallet had fallen to the floor, and went over to tell him so, to his effusive thanks. Later, as he headed to the bathroom, he clapped me on the shoulder: "I *really* appreciate that!" "It gave me a chance to say something to you, " I said, daringly. When he came back from the men's room, he got his coat off the stool he'd been on and left, leaving me certain I'd spooked him. I'd arrived feeling tanned and smart in my new blue and white striped T-shirt, fresh from the gym—felt something of the old spirit, saw myself being checked out by guys as I walked in. It crossed my mind now that I might be like Aunt Pittypat, batting my eyes and feeling like a rushed girl, and looking like an old man. "I've forgotten how to be *cute*," I told Gina.

August 8, 1994

Letter from the Clinic Study on Friday with a fact sheet on "Non-Progressives." Of 552 men in the study who've been HIV+ for ten years or more, 7% remain with T-cells above 500 (or "healthy")—mine being 1300 in March; 72% have AIDS or have died. There's a little pie chart, which makes me picture the wedge as it shrinks, with that 7% of us scrambling to stay on our diminishing slice.

September 25, 1994

A literary weekend, this has been, while Leather Week and the Folsom Street Fair played out in the background. I met Gina straight from Riddley on Friday and we headed for Van Ness

Street, ate dinner, and went to hear Ned Rorem at the Herbst (whose memoir, *Knowing When to Stop*, I'd been reading happily all week), interviewed by Wayne Koestenbaum. Gina and I saw Ned together at the Herbst in November '87—she remembers me calling home before it began to check on Jack, who was sick, but hadn't yet plummeted.

Ned was delightful, handsome, full of spontaneous-sounding bon mots and aphorisms ("unhappiness is only for the young"), with his head tossing, and his endearing speech impediment. Wayne was skinnier than his jacket photos, wiry-haired, elfish, clad in a majorette jacket, odd black velvet pants with little silver buttons going up the legs, and a ruffled shirt, like an elevator operator in Mod London. He had a raspy, whispery voice and asked good questions, though Ned firmly side-stepped sex and his legendary beauty as topics of discussion.

November 19, 1994
Last Sunday as I was wandering the aisles at Walgreen's in the Castro looking for shampoo, I rounded a corner and there was Matt Galante. He was wearing earphones, shuffling along in baggy dark plaid shorts. I said hello. What followed was mostly comical, and doesn't seem to have re-infected me with any feverish need for him. He talked as if he hadn't had anyone to talk to in a year: thinks of me often, wants to call, is afraid I'd hang up (I would have). I felt cool and collected but, turning

to have my items rung up, the coat under my arm knocked over a pyramid of cheap perfumes which cascaded around us, some landing upended and spraying nasty fragrances.

He followed me out. "Are you hurrying somewhere? Could we get coffee and talk?" We went to Pasqua. His version of "the ending": he was about to really get involved with me when I brutally cut him off. I overturned my latte and drenched my pants leg. "Come to my house for some shorts…" "No thanks!" He walked alongside me as I headed toward Pearl Street. Was I seeing anyone? No, I haven't been with anyone since we stopped seeing each other. This was immediately garbled into: he'd hurt me so badly, I'd retreated into celibacy—a great shame, because I'm so good in bed. Didn't we have great sex?

That evening I put down my book and walked around the corner to the feeble neighborhood leather bar, Motorwerks (guess that's the Dutch spelling) for a beer. Several paunchy, bearded bear-types in leather baseball caps stood around puffing cigars as if someone had just gotten a promotion or had a baby. One of them sauntered over, sat down beside me, and began telling me excitedly about how he'd been painting his apartment, buying new furniture, choosing new carpet. Opposite us, up at the bar, I watched a frail and very drunk sixty-something-year-old man being bullied by his slightly younger, bearded friend: "Jody! You whore! Judy! Jody! Get over here! Wanna drink? Wanna piece of ass? Whore!"

Judy/Jody just cringed and smiled and bobbed his head, and I
thought of Lucky on the end of his rope in *Waiting for Godot*.

November 21, 1994
Came home about 11:00 P.M., leashed the dog, and started
down the block. Sometime after Henry'd peed for the third
time on a piece of crumpled newspaper, I heard footsteps on
the other side of the street. I looked over, expecting to see one
of my neighbors, or a street person, and saw a tall, youngish
man in the sort of thigh-length black leather car coat you only
used to see on straight black dudes. He was looking over at
me, leering really; despite its coming completely out of
nowhere, there was no doubt what this guy was up to, and I
felt flustered and yet cocky from all the wine and laughing at
dinner with Louise and Riddley pal Melanie. I continued along
with the dog; young X turned and stared after, then crossed
the street and started down the block ahead of me. Henry was
straining at the leash; I let go and he raced up to the leather-
coated youth and jumped at his legs. He was standing at the
foot of the steps to my apartment. As I reached him, he looked
at me with a crooked smile, an erection visibly poking up in
his baggy jeans—and I realized this was serious. He was thin
and hard-bodied, with short reddish hair, and raw-looking
Irish immigrant features. I grinned back at him: "What're you
up to?" He looked at me and reached to rub my crotch.

"Wanna come up?" I said, jerking my head toward the lit bay windows. He nodded. When we were inside, I turned and stopped him on the stairs. If he wouldn't kiss me, I decided, that was it, I wouldn't take the risk. I pulled his head toward me, and he kissed me brusquely, shoving his tongue in my mouth and bumping my forehead, taking my hand and pressing it to his boner. I decided he wasn't a serial killer, and in we went. I was just slightly drunk; this probably wouldn't have happened if I'd been perfectly sober.

Inside, he took a jerky look around as he pulled off his coat—with sheer indifference, I thought. He was clearly here for one urgent purpose. He started undoing my belt and unzipping my pants; I yanked off my T-shirt and began opening his ludicrously oversized jeans. Surprise! He was wearing tight, black boxer-length Marky Mark underwear that pinned his long hard-on sideways. He'd barely said a word, though something he uttered as I tugged at his jeans ("Cheers"? "Tah"?) reinforced my Irish impression. When I yanked down his trendy underwear, his long reddish dick jerked upward toward his hard belly, which he'd exposed, pulling his T-shirt up above his flat red nipples. I took hold of his dick, sniffed it, sat back on my haunches and admired it. "You have a beautiful dick," I said. He made no answer, but bucked his hips, thrusting into my fist. I didn't realize till I'd pulled back to stare, jacking it slowly—the very red, funky-smelling head, the looser, moveable skin that felt to my fingers like moving a chamois over a base-ball bat—he was uncircumsized.

I took it in my mouth. He grunted and pumped. I'd been a bit stunned out of reality; now, as I sucked—tasting and smelling this hard, urgent cock—I came more and more into focus, stopping to reach under and feel his hard, skinny ass, to move down and lick his red balls, snuffle behind, stare at the pale coppery pubic hair—reach up to stroke his hairless chest. We both had our shoes on, pants shoved down to our ankles; he'd sat on the side of the bed and fallen back. I climbed up and crouched with my erection waving in his face. "You want to suck it?" He turned his head aside, but reached up to inex-pertly jack it. Was he "straight"? Or being safe-sex careful? I went gladly back to sucking his cock, and he soon moaned, pulled my head away, and lay shivering a moment. I thought it decent of him not to just shoot his wad in my mouth—but I decided without a qualm that I wanted to feel just that: his cum jetting on my tongue. I wanted to taste him. I slowly sucked just the velvety head of his pink dick. He thrashed and groaned, gripped my head hard, and shuddered—and my mouth was flooded with the pungent, herby, sharp, so-much-missed taste of hot cum. I spit it into my hand and wiped it on the spread, a halfway measure. I felt self-conscious as I went back to jerking myself off, sniffing and sucking his softening cock. I knew I'd never come if I sensed he was boredly waiting for me to finish.

I surfaced and looked him in the eye: "You don't have to wait around for me if you don't want to…." Whatever his story was, he had a certain code of behavior because, without saying anything, he indicated I should continue. This encouraged me to ask for what I wanted. "Could you stand up so I can get a better look at your ass?" He stood, awkwardly, with his pants and underwear still jammed around his ankles, and helpfully hiked his T-shirt up again. He had a long, slender but muscled back, and a compact, hard, white butt. My dick sprang back to an urgent boner as I kissed his pale cheeks, sniffed the crack (soap and sweat) and licked it lightly, and finally pushed my face between his tight buttocks and tenderly kissed his clenched asshole, which instantly relaxed against my lips—and I shot copiously across the carpet, as my silent guest cannily stepped aside to avoid having his pants and shoes sprayed with my cum.

He immediately pulled up his pants, tucked in his shirt, and pulled on his slightly smelly black leather car coat, and swiveled his head looking for the door, which I stepped to and opened. "Cheers," I said as he hurried out, and he nodded, blankly.

December 24, 1994
Friday, off work, I went to lunch with Gina at Anchor Oyster Bar and then we met Tom Ace at Pasqua to collect my first copies of the new *Diseased Pariah News* with my story

"Widow Hopper" in it. That Tom's terrifically cute added to the general excitement as we gaped at the ink-reeking 'zine in the hopping X-mas-crowded coffee bar. Something I said caused Tom to put his arm around me and give me a comradely squeeze, which was very pleasant. He admitted authorship of the latest bus shelter advertising alteration: the "Mr. Jenkins" Tanqueray gin ad at Eighteenth and Diamond, on which the original letters have been cunningly rearranged to read *Mr. Jenkins' mouth hungers for ass when he sips too much Tanqueray*. 'Course his urban pranksterism only adds to the appeal of the rock-climbing bod, blue eyes, lank blond hair, and John Malkovich nose.

1995

January 8, 1995

Go—you may call it madness, folly;

You shall not chase my gloom away.

There's such a charm in melancholy,

I would not, if I could, be gay.

—*Poems*, Samuel Rogers, 1816

Browsing through some pretty, moldering old books among the stacks Richard gave me, I came across this lyric in the obscure *Rogers's Poems*.

Dinner with Bob Thursday night. He was glum about news that Scott Taylor had died. This was the friendly former porn star I met when I was out celebrating my promotion last March. Taylor was famous for ranting at the audience at live sex shows at the Nob Hill, and, among others, a porn film called *Dr. Dick*, in which he takes ever-larger objects from a medical bag and inserts them into his penis.

January 24, 1995

Tall, slim, nicely-built redhead I've noticed lately at the gym seemed to be staring at me last evening while I worked out. Maybe he reminds me slightly of my Pearl Street pickup of a couple months ago—though he's much more attractive. After showering, he turned up beside me at the lockers, naked and drying off a few feet away, looking back at me. This was the first time I'd glimpsed his dick: it's thick as a tree trunk, very red, and seemed to be in a state of partial erection over someone. He pulled on some black bikini underwear, then pants and a pullover that belied a taste similar to that of my street amour (dark red plaid pants—but tight over his hard ass—and a multi-colored, striped, V-neck thing: a high school coach's garb—all he lacked was the clipboard and a whistle on a cord around his neck). He looked full of himself, and if he's the same short-red-haired guy who drove me out of the sauna on Thursday with his loud political oration, he's some kind of gay Republican ninny. I was so stricken by his glancing in my direction while his hand carelessly brushed his cock, I walked out slowly, imagining him following me, and thought of him the rest of the evening, well after jacking off feverishly the moment I walked in the door.

January 25, 1995
A voicemail at work on Monday, and then faxed instructions yesterday from Winston Wilde about calling a small portion of the phone tree when Paul Monette dies, which is apparently imminent. A list of unacceptable phrases, surely dictated by Paul: "He's passed on, in a better place, with God now..."

February 13, 1995

Yesterday, Gina and I drove with Bob to Martha's in Oakland for Nora's second birthday party. Nora darted around in blue rubber boots and a Bullwinkle bib chattering, as she's begun to do since Thanksgiving. "Happy birthday to *me!*" she'd crow winningly, then look around beaming. I was remembering how excited Richard was when we heard Martha was pregnant—and how, only a few months later, I lost it completely when I glanced behind me during his memorial and saw Bob and a very pregnant Martha clinging to each other and sobbing.

We drove back by way of U. C. Berkeley museum for a gay art exhibit, "In a Different Light," noting throngs of cute boys on Shattuck peddling by on bikes, round butts in the air, young, and one assumes, full of cum. Back in the city, Gina had to be dropped off before her mother went bonkers and started smashing up the furnishings of her basement lair. I'd given Gina a birthday/Valentine's Day card with a drawing of a Victorian skeleton key: *You hold the key to my heart.* "Course there are several dupes in circulation," I added.

Bob and I went on to dinner. "Do you suppose we'll ever have sex again?" I asked. "*You* will," he said.

June 26, 1995

A week ago I lay reading sleepily, a Trollope biography denting my chest, when the phone trilled, the machine clicked on, and

I dreamily listened to Matt, whom I'd spoken to at the Herbst Theater David Sedaris reading, reciting his whereabouts for the following day: "I hope you'll call me soon." I lay thinking about whether to drift off to sleep or get up and call back. I knew if I called now I'd probably tell the truth. I went to the couch in my underwear, in the half-light, and called. "I felt very attracted to you the other night. How much of it is simply physical desperation I don't know." (This last must have stung, and probably wasn't nice, but it's true. Would I feel this way if I were seeing someone else?)

"I know, I was feeling horny for you," he said. "I wanted to try something the last time I saw you."

Saturday, I walked over to Matt's in the evening heat. He was washing glasses from his cocktail party the night before. I sat at the kitchen table; his frayed cat, Pies, was spread across the cool of a large ceramic serving dish glaring at me. When Matt finished his dishes, he stepped over and stood in front of me and began massaging my shoulders, his skinny brown legs sticking out of some old swimming trunks. He'd cut his hair very short that day because of the heat. I pulled him closer, nuzzling his chest. Both our dicks were already hard and jutting out. We pulled off our shirts and moved into the other room and lay on the futon. He solemnly took my hard-on into his mouth and started sucking and I thought: *Nearly two years, it's been*. We ended up lying face to face, each grasping the other's cock, slick with sweat, saliva, and lube, and I was kissing his lips, face and head and breathing in his breath, and we came thrusting into each other's wet fists.

We showered and sat with drinks in the little backyard space behind his studio. I brought up his old "I don't want a boyfriend" mantra. "That's changed. But I'm still the same *person*," he warned.

"Do you love me?" I wanted to know—or rather, to make him say. It seems clear he does, in some way.

"Of course," he answered, coolly.

July 4, 1995

Last night, after drinks with George, Riddley House friend I've cajoled into doing the five-week Kenny Fries poetry workshop with me, I was hailed by Tim Morrow in front of Twin Peaks. He was out for a lone walk, duded up in tight jeans, blue work shirt and cowboy boots. I see him now and then at the gym, so I've slowly gotten used to him as merely a familiar face in the present, and not the magically resurfaced romantic encounter of the past. (We tricked in March of '81 when he was visiting from the East Coast on spring break. He was an adorable, cocky little twenty-one-year-old runner with curly black hair, olive skin, and a Boston accent. It was the last night of his week in San Francisco. We went back to his hotel, the suitably named Brothel, and fucked and talked all night. We

wrote and called for several years after that, then lost touch—
till I picked up a *BAR* one day last year and saw his picture—
bearded, less hair, but still an attractive man—beside a review
of an HIV law book he'd written, and I phoned him up. We
met, but it didn't lead anywhere.)

The workshop excitement and two glasses of wine under
my belt made me confident and candid and I didn't shrug off
his enthusiastic embrace. "Come have a drink," I said. We
walked to Moby Dick and sat side by side on stools. He was all
smiles: "You look good." I quizzed him: Why does he act so
thrilled when we meet, but has never called? Did he really just
join my gym after he found out I went there? Did he have a
hairy back when we tricked in '81? (He does now, I've seen him
in the shower.) Is he still attracted to me, or not? (Yes, but I
move too fast.) Would he mind kissing me now? The answer to
this was some serious public necking, which may have shocked
the couple of elderly, disco-traumatized tropical fish treading
water in the tank behind the bar, but no one else, as the place
was almost empty. To my surprise, he aggressively thrust his
tongue in my mouth. I got an erection, and sat back dizzily,
scrutinizing his smiling face. Tim's features have sharpened, but
I could easily see the passionate boy from the Brothel. But he
didn't say, "Let's go back to my place," and I know he'll slap
me on the back or come up behind me and snap my jock and
continue on his way the next time we meet at the gym.

July 18, 1995

It's been a week of unusual sweltering hot weather. Thursday at work Lisa and I took our lunch over to the pier with Isaac, and I took my shirt off as we sat baking on a park bench, gulls screeching and hanging in the clear air in front of us. Isaac acted all flustered and reached to tweak my nipple. He was leaving for a business trip that afternoon, and I said he should be sure to come by my office and say good-bye before then. A few hours later he stepped in, looking cute and rosy (he's generally pale) from the lunchtime sun, wearing a red-plaid shirt. He inanely went over his schedule while I felt my dick hardening and wondered how I could maneuver kissing him. The back wall of my office is graced with a frosted glass window onto a seldom-trod hall; there's a wall of the same opaque glass opposite, alongside the door. "C'mere," I said, standing up and pulling him behind the half-open door. "I want to kiss you good-bye."

"Ohhh, that's sweet," he said, in his kindergarten-teacher voice, and came forward to give me a little hug. I kissed him, at first awkwardly, then I felt him realizing I intended more— how quickly he must have had to weigh his decision—and he opened his lips and we really made out for a moment.

July 26, 1995

When I called Matt about getting together we ended up having a long, eye-opening talk. I'm mistaken, he says, in remembering any statements from him about things being different this time—he doesn't have romantic feelings like other people; sex is just something you do, not a big personal deal. "I'm still seeing the guy I was seeing before you came back on the scene, and I've had sex with other people since you and I have been dating. Don't forget, you had twenty years of sex with whoever you liked!" As Matt is less than five years younger than me, I'm not sure how I'm supposed to have gotten this twenty-year jump on him.

Still, I headed over at the appointed time and we embraced without mention of the earlier conversation. "Can we just get undressed instead of wrestling each piece off as we go?" I asked, and soon we were naked and I was lying atop him and we were swept off into frantic, panting sex. In the end he was slouched sitting up on the futon and I was crouched with my thighs tightly grasping his chest, one hand holding the back of his head, fucking him in the mouth till I yanked out to shoot and he sprayed my back with his cum at the same time. This is where whatever's between us begins and ends; how can he deny it?

July 31, 1995
Saturday night Isaac and I went to dinner and *Medea, The Musical.* Afterward, we sat in a little café and talked about the inadvisability of our having sex, since we work so near each

other. "Well, there's another piece in all this I haven't talked to you about: Jim, who I'm seeing tomorrow." (He has a first date with someone he's met online.) During this level-headed discussion, we both got visible boners, and he jumped up and untucked his shirt to hide his. I spread my legs and let him look. "Just kiss me, then," I said, and he finally did, briefly, and it was hot.

When he'd driven me home, he pulled into the driveway and turned off the motor, "to talk," which of course meant we were wildly making out in seconds. I was kissing the cool back of his neck, reaching up his shirt to play with his nipples. For a while, he yanked my hand away every time I reached for his dick; then, at some point I took his hand and put it on my straining hard-on, and he started rubbing it, and then I was freely rubbing the very sizeable lump at his crotch.

It was all very exciting, yet I began to feel a bit duped: If we weren't going to do it, why keep building back up to it and stopping? It dawned on me later: Isaac's ambitious, he has lots of plans, he wants to have kids—he may not want to risk even having safe sex with me. I have the luxury of almost forgetting about my HIV status, thanks to my long-time nonprogressor situation. Other than not depositing my cum inside anyone, I don't think about it. There's no reason he shouldn't feel the way he does, and honestly, I can't say I want to marry him and adopt babies. Still, it stings.

August 2, 1995

To Matt's Friday night, after not meeting all week. After several glasses of wine he informed me he thought he might be up to anal sex, and soon I was slipping on a ribbed condom and sticking my cock up his ass.

Later, on the subject of white chest hairs (I'd explained my experimental clipping of my chest for that reason), Matt explained he doesn't mind them himself; after all, *they just mean he's that much closer to death.* (This was said through a lungful of cigarette smoke, very Anne Sexton.)

August 28, 1995

I spent four hours Sunday evening rambling South of Market with Nate. We met at the Eagle beer bust, then walked over to his new favorite spot, the Hole in the Wall, a so-called gay biker bar. Sleazy it was, decorated like the old Stud with weird, trippy objects mounted on the walls and ceiling, and with a black-lit back room area. Several pot-bellied, bosomy older gents ambled in and out of the bathroom clad only in shoes. We moved to stand beside a young grunge-styled guy Nate had been eyeing, a recent arrival from Seattle: neck-length hair, scarf tied dew-rag fashion over his head, leather motorcycle jacket, ripped cutoffs (muscular legs), and boots. A well-built guy, dressed more for the Giraffe in khakis and Lacoste, came up and gave me a big squeeze, claiming we'd met, though I'm sure I'd never seen him before in my life. He was hot, but too weird—too sure of himself in an attractive but nervous-making way, taking my hand and placing it on his semi-erect dick. I kissed him once, why not? while Mr. Seattle looked on approvingly. Then a cute guy plonked down on the ledge beside me and my suitor was feeling us both up at once, and I ceased to encourage him—he seemed like an ant dragging crumbs back to his lair.

Nate disappeared for twenty minutes with a hot guy who walked by and grabbed his arm, leaving me to chat with the affable grunge-boy, who was, I think, let down by Nate's defection. The subject of reading arose, and he beamed—he loves to read, reads all the time. He's currently reading a really good Dean Koontz novel. Now my interest abated.

September 2, 1995
The dead come marching two by two, hurrah, hurrah. *Anastasia*-like dream last night in which Gary and Michael had returned looking older, altered, both claiming to have only faked their deaths. Gary emptied an envelope full of photographs out on the table—all old snapshots of us together I'd forgotten about, till now. "I've written about you," I said.

"We know."

Broke up with Matt again, this time for good.

September 9, 1995

Dinner out with Gina last night, then, after she'd sped away in a cab, a walk by Giraffe for a drink. Turns out the amorous buff guy from the previous Sunday at the Hole in the Wall is a sometime DJ there. He appeared in front of me, grabbed my legs and kissed me. "Oh, I went home by myself that night," he claimed, when I took him to task for his fickle behavior. I went back to the DJ booth with him, feeling a bit tipsy, and daydreamed while he rattled off boring details about how one dubs tapes and videos, blah blah. (*If I tricked with him, he might show me how to set my VCR*, I thought idly.) We knelt below the window and made out some more. I admitted to having reservations about doing it with him; my impression is that he'd be too insistent about sticking his (apparent) monster dick in me. "I'd have to think about that for a while," I said. He said something crude about a previous trick and "packing fudge" that put me right off him, and when I looked out the window and spotted Nate sitting by himself at the bar, I decided to descend from DJ Olympus and went out to join him.

"You don't go to Rome to meet Japanese men," Isaac said at lunch yesterday—that is, if what you really want is monogamous love, don't expect to find it with a promiscuous man met at the Hole in the Wall. Yes, but—

September 23, 1995

"He was one of those men who at forty looks thirty but who will perhaps in a few days look fifty."—Scott Spencer, *Men in Black*

Who needs Dean Koontz when you can read a line as chilling as this in Scott Spencer? It's the second of my three days in Forestville at the little rental cottage on a hill above a nice old turn-of-the-century farmhouse, where Matt and I stayed in June of '93. This time I'm on my own. I had the entire place to myself all afternoon—sunned, reading the new Lytton Strachey biography, pulling off my blue gym shorts to swim laps naked in the nice big pool on the lawn in front of the main house. Later, Pavel, the owner, pulled up in his truck, shirtless and looking awfully cute with his curly dark hair, hairy chest, and Sonoma tan, came down and chatted, then went up to sweep the big veranda. I jumped in the pool again and swam up and down. Just as I was climbing out, Pavel appeared again: "Temptress!" he said. "I guess I'll go in..." and he pulled off his shorts, stood there for a bit talking (so I could take a good look? I did), then plunged in and swam briefly, jumped out and put his shorts back on. He pulled a chaise up near mine and asked me what I thought the jury would do in the OJ trial. (I believe I may actually never have had a conversation on this topic till now.) Then his cell phone twittered and he remained on the patio talking, one assumes, to his new lover, who hasn't been on the scene while I've been here. He laughed: "I knew you were going to say that!" then lowered his voice. No, he hasn't fucked the guest, I'm sorry to say.

December 23, 1995

After I'd recounted the doomed fix-up Gina attempted last week, meeting me for drinks with a gay pal from her office—he'd seen me in her vacation photos and made inquiries—Bob told me sagely at dinner: "You have to get used to the idea that you're older now, and you may have to do the pursuing."

"No!" I cried. "Not pursue!"

1996

January 20, 1996

A package from one of my favorite Riddley authors arrived on Thursday, the day before my birthday, with a little handmade book for a birthday card. The illustrations depict a skinny, specs-wearing figure who looks like me saying a regretful farewell to a hunky, blond, and glowing youth, who carries all the light and color away with him as he disappears over a hill. Then, after a frame of dejection, a crown rises up from behind the hill and settles on "Kevin's" head, and he's in color, instead of black and gray, and looks a bit more fetching, if mature. I gather I'm to cease regretting my youth and assume my tiara of wisdom.

February 22, 1996 (New York)

In Manhattan for four days to train the East Coast assistant to Rudolph, the editor I'm soon to wait upon in the new, reduced scheme of things at Riddley. Excruciating days sitting with Rudolph's lackadaisical helper in their isolated 29th floor office trying to make the day move while time stalls and drags—knowing my real work's piling up on my desk back at home. I pretended to myself it wasn't so awful so I wouldn't go screaming mad and went padding along from one ominously

253

moaning elevator bank to another, greasy-feeling and dowdy in awkward wrinkled shirts and hateful tie. The morning after a boozy dinner with my cousin and her girlfriend, I thought the skyscraper was swaying and nearly keeled over while standing in the lobby listening to a speech from an ancient editor who'd been given some award.

Lunching at a trendy restaurant yesterday with Rudolph and a gorgon of an agent whose food kept flying from her mouth and onto my plate and, I swear, right into my water glass once, I turned my head and, in a sort of *Simpsons* moment, stared at the large head of Ed Koch, who was seated directly behind me. That afternoon, scoping out East-West Books, I watched Marsha Mason in a jogging suit asking for books and tapes on Tibetan chant, while one stranger after another tip-toed up to say, "I just so admire your *work*."

The next day I attended the New York editorial meeting— quite intimidating, far more curt and formal than our cracker barrel chats. Rudolph dragged me around to try and schmooze— his word—with editors afterward, which was humiliating, as they clearly scorn him. I had little to say, and they seemed either baffled at our intrusion or downright unfriendly.

February 23, 1996 (Boston)
Hiding in my room at OutWrite, the gay writers' conference. If this were a bar, which it is in a way, I'd have bolted and run

by now. I'm exhausted at the thought of facing 2,000 sharp-eyed queens, an unsightly bump on my forehead from all the past week's stress disfiguring whatever looks I have. Talk about water, water everywhere: there're appealing gay men interested in writing and publishing at every turn, and nobody so much as glancing at me—except for Craig Lucas, who was trying to find the end of the line for the bar behind me at the cocktail reception awhile ago and was disarmingly friendly. We talked about the weird hotel air and then I focused on his nametag and gulped (writing *Betty Rubble, Bedrock Books* on mine now seemed a mistake). I told him how much I'd admired his "Postcard from Grief" in the *Advocate* last summer, but was struck quite dumb after that.

March 3, 1996
Yesterday was clear and warm after a cold rainy week, with the automatic lift of spirits the sun brings. I'd been browsing the *BAR* personals to scope out the competition, but instead saw one I wanted to call. I dialed this guy's mailbox and said something, probably all the wrong things. Then, natch, I imagined every time I came in the message light would be blinking. Maybe he's simply away pedaling a mountain bike somewhere. For a while I was all "up," certain I was on the verge of some new development, instead of looking at the date on the *Examiner* and thinking: *three years, two months, and ten*

days since Richard died; seven years, eight months, and three days since Jack. Not so fast, cowboy.

March 5, 1996

I've stalled for the moment about placing my own ad, not getting called back by the one *I* called having taken the wind out of my sails.

On the other hand, Sunday's adventure, though fruitless, overall brought me up a bit—I think I could try Eros again at a more ambitious time. I'd gone into the steam room and sat on a top ledge; pretty soon there were about six to eight guys spread about, mostly fiddling with their dicks to get them hard. A rather fat, mean-looking fellow sat against the wall to my left with his arms crossed over his stomach; a young, longish-haired guy—hot body—sat just below me stroking his dick, which quickly grew erect; to my right, quite close, a nondescript thirty-something guy, shag hairdo, short beard, and a horse face, looked at me and—yes—stroked his short, fat dick. The steam came on periodically with a noisy blast and when it stopped and you could see again, people had made their moves: somebody was sucking dick on the other side of horsey; hippie, his mouth hanging open, was jacking the impassive fat guy's hard-on. I half-heartedly groped horsey's big-headed shorty, which he allowed, just, but turned his head away from kissing, and he removed his hand as if from a hot stove when he found

I was only half-erect. My problem: I get hard from someone's interest, implied or physical, but I can't just get an erection for a general audience and wait for comers. And then I'd been in the scalding steam room for twenty minutes and my heart was racing and my dick did not leap to its customary position when I bent to suck horsey's cock. I halted a bit awkwardly, and horsey seemed so uninterested in me—horsey thought I was what, piggy?—I left to get some air. I wandered the dark cul-de-sacs upstairs—nobody stopped in his tracks for me. One wiry, dark-haired guy caught my eye, but hurried on. It was like a nightmare airport, and I didn't know my gate.

March 31, 1996
Weird gun-metal-blue rain clouds spread over the east horizon, sultry almost, the sun shining hot through the gaps. I walk home down Market Street, shaky-legged, oiled up and slick as a seal, jaunty, drinking a tropical protein shake through a straw. Thirty minutes earlier, a pink, fat dick with a gold ring through the tip was pulsing in my mouth. I feel tired and emotionally raw now. It's love and the aftermath of sex I want too, of course, so I'm a little sad at the same time as I'm exhilarated and sated.

I'd decided yesterday to call and book a massage with this guy whose ad in the massage section of *BAR* appealed to me; he looked attractive, nicely built, and comfortable, like he wouldn't be all weird and creepy about the sex part.

The first thing I noticed when he buzzed me into the second floor Victorian flat and leaned smiling over the banister was that his short hair and goatee, dark in the ad, were now blond or reddish-orange. He showed me into a room set up with burning scented candle, boring new age music, and a professional massage table with the towel-padded keyhole at one end to stick your face in.

I hadn't asked over the phone, though his being casually naked in the ad had seemed to indicate so, if this was sexual or nonsexual; I asked now. "It can be," he said, smiling. "It depends on the client, and how I feel." I got hard just taking my pants off, but he began with me on my stomach, so I didn't have to worry about that immediately. He gave a long, thorough, strong-handed massage, really digging between the tightened muscles in the backs of my legs and shoulders. When he ran his fingers down my arms and laced his hand through mine in that way they do, tears sprang to my eyes. I realized how I've ached for that kind of touch as well.

By the time he asked me to turn over I was quite jellied, and no longer had a raging erection, but when he touched the insides of my thighs, boom—my dick shot to attention. He'd been using lotion all along, and after maybe twenty minutes of working on my legs and arms, he ran his fingers lightly up the shaft of my dick, put more lotion on his hand, and began to jack the head.

I was shaking; I felt like I was going to fly off the table. I moaned discretely and started thrusting into his fist, opening my eyes and looking up at him. Unlike in the ad, he was clad in some loose swimming trunks and a tank top. I reached around and cupped his very nice round ass, and began reaching up the open legs of his shorts and stroking his sweaty crack. He pulled off the tank top. I palmed his chest and touched his pinkish nipples but didn't pinch them, unsure of the boundaries. He was rubbing his crotch, clearly hard, against my side.

"Can I touch your cock?" I asked politely. He stepped out of the trunks and went back to pumping my dick, bending and sucking the head with that sloppy, smutty popping sound, and suddenly a fully erect, upward curving, fat white cock—with, yes, a gold ring through the dripping glans—was bobbing in my face. I sniffed, kissed, and then took it into my mouth and sucked enthusiastically, the ring clicking as it passed my front teeth. Now he was moaning, and deep-throating my cock unabashedly. I reached into the wet crack of his ass and stroked his silky-haired chest. "I'm going to come—" he breathed, and I made a quick judgment call ("Cinderella *shall* go to the ball!") and continued blowing him till he ejaculated copiously in my mouth and I shot dramatically past my head in four or five porn-quality jets, my butt arched off the table. He actually continued the massage, doing my face and chest—and then went away and returned with wet, hot towels with which he wiped me down from head to toe.

I emerged feeling euphoric, trembling, strange—because I'd been made so vulnerable and then ejected back out into my single life with a hug at the door.

April 12, 1996
Dreamt this, last night: I was sitting in a theater waiting for a play to start and there was Jack's friend Charlie, who died last November, sitting beside me. When I looked over and stared at him, well aware of why his being there was so surprising, he smiled and *beamed* at me, and I put my hand on his chest, then over his terribly thin, gnarled hand. I must have stuttered out something like "So, there *is* an afterlife?"

"Oh yeah," he said, nonchalantly.

"So then you've seen Jack?"

"Sure," he said, like he'd just left him at the corner. "He's very worried about who you're going to be with...."

April 18, 1996
Ninety years post-Great Quake this morning. The afternoon paper will have a photo of some very old people spraying a new coat of gold paint on that Dolores Park hydrant that saved the Mission.

Speaking of earthshaking, I agonized over and finally called in and recorded my mailbox greeting last evening. Just now I called and listened to it and I sound nasal, hesitant, hopeless. *BAR* comes out today with my ad: *books and sex— are reasons to live.*

April 27, 1996

Arranged to meet Jerry for a beer yesterday at 5:00. Earlier in the week he'd left a long, sensible message reacting to some of what I'd said in my ad—which made him stand out from the more typical ones left by men with slurry voices and ice cubes chattering in highball glasses in the background.

I was first to show, which meant I had to sit in the sunny window at Pilsner's wondering each time a cute or awful figure came through the door, "Is this him?" And then someone walked up saying, "You wouldn't be Kevin, would you?" He wore a sort of baggy Lacoste shirt and Levis; he was 'older,' that is, he had a lined face, graying pale brown hair, pretty eyes (blue?)—looked like he'd been outdoors a lot. He had a tendency to squint several times quickly in succession. He was nicer than his phone voice.

We went to dinner. He mentioned having a spiritual teacher, "Omni Ra," whose goofy-jacketed books I remember selling at Bonanza Books (didn't one have a psychedelic gorilla wearing a party hat on the front?). But he didn't spout spacey new age stuff. I wasn't sure of my physical attraction, but thought it worth a try; I asked, sitting back here on the couch after dinner, would he like to neck a bit?—and he "reluctantly" agreed, and then of course we were going to town. He'd hauled my hard-on out, and I reached for his, and hooray!— it was of a good size and hard. When I came, it was one of those shotgun blasts.

May 7, 1996

Met Paul, whose Italian last name I can't recall, on Wednesday night next to Clean Well-Lighted Place for Books before the reading I felt duty-bound to attend (my work on this particular book consisted chiefly of leaving the author endless messages hounding him for the overdue manuscript). Paul's also forty, dark, husky, and hairy; gold chain, ring, fancy watch, fancy boxer shorts—looks like a sexy middle-aged straight Italian man. A bit taciturn, which seems part of his butch nature. Nice blue eyes and a handsome smile.

We had only a moment to talk before hurrying over to the reading; as we wove through browsers I pulled him into an alcove between two bookcases and told him, much-abreviatedly, of Monday's nightmare meeting with Bachelor #3, when I'd knocked over my chair fleeing the human Gila-monster who'd been spitting on his hand and grooming himself. "If that's how you're seeing me, you can escape right now and no hard feelings—"

"That's not what I'm feeling," he said, smiling sexily, and pulling me against him.

May 13, 1996

The Jerry thing has ended awkwardly. Essentially he's a pleasant, fairly intelligent person, but he's not, and the sex isn't,
what I'd want all the time. He's totally into *my* dick, sucking
and jerking me off, which is nice in a purely selfish way, but not
enough emotionally. I didn't fall in love with him at first sight,
and I never could. There's a certain occasional saccharine tone
("You're a beautiful man.... Mmmm, I love the direction this is
going in!") that made me sure deep down this couldn't go on.
For chrissakes, his license plate says "LUV4RA!"

In the midst of the last slow, sparsely populated, surreal
waiting-for-layoffs afternoon at Riddley today, I thought of
Paul, the guy I spent Friday and Saturday nights with, and
found myself having a surprising rush of feeling for him. I
never, not for a second, had a natural, emotional feeling like
that with Jerry. I'd expected to be thinking, *Great, Paul's off
for his previously planned three weeks in Europe, leaving me
free to size up the remaining "bachelors,"* but instead I feel sad
that he's leaving.

May 29, 1996

The Sunday evening of little brother Mark's first weekend
here, Rick Jimenez (Bachelor #2) came with Bob and us to
see Blossom Dearie. Rick's a tall, olive-skinned Latino,
slightly fey, but sexily rangy at the same time. At the Great

American Music Hall, while Mark and Bob roamed for a closer stage view, Mr. Jimenez and I held hands and groped. (I got an erection in baggy jeans and put his hand on it; he set about pressing and squeezing it, while staring toward the little wizened woman with a pixie cut warbling "Peel Me a Grape.") Oddly, though, he evaded my attempts to kiss him in the backseat later; if he considers kissing unsafe, there's a problem.

Paul returns from Europe in a week, and that may heat up to a degree that will preclude other contenders. Today a post-card from Paris: he went to Père Lachaise and gave my regards to Oscar, as I'd requested (and ran into two queens from his gym on his way from Oscar to Gertrude).

June 2, 1996

Movie with Rick. We'd talked on the phone the night before. "I've got a kind of quandary." Seems someone he'd dated who wouldn't make a commitment has now decided (with me as stalking horse?) to "make a commitment." As I'm privately counting the days till Paul's return, I could hardly be put out. I explained that I was dating others as well and not to give it another thought. We went to dinner and a stupid alien movie he chose (having nixed *Cold Comfort Farm*).

Afterward, he moaned about his long drive back to Concord, so I said, not thinking he'd accept, well, you're welcome to sleep over on the couch or whatever. When he promptly said yes, I realized he wanted to try it on with me after all. (The boyfriend to whom he's freshly committed is out of town.) When we got into bed, stripped to jockeys, he placed himself against me, and after about ten seconds, made a big show of pulling off his underwear beneath the sheets ("I'm so *hot!*"). *OK*, I thought, *me too*, and tossed my own on the rug. Then followed a bizarre cock tease the likes of which I haven't encountered since—well, since last July, parked out front at 2:00 A.M. necking with Isaac in his car. He'd rub his size-large boner against my butt and brush his hand over my aching erection, but when I reached for his dick or attempted to roll over and kiss him, he'd stop me: "Oh, you're really trying to tempt me, I don't want to do this—" Then, ten minutes later, as I drifted off to sleep, his hand was back on my cock.

I sat up and turned on the light. "Look, do you want to have sex, or do you want to go to sleep?"

"No, I told you, I can't have sex with you, I *promised*." But all night long I woke to him lightly stroking my dick, keeping it hot and hard. Around 4:00 A.M. I woke from a sexual dream to find him jacking me off in earnest, and I rolled over and enjoyed it, finally ejaculating so intensely it burned on the way out. I jacked him off then, sucking and biting his nipples while he whined, "No, I can't, stop, I mustn't." (I thought this kind of "You're bad, we mustn't" rap went out with Lana, the older girl I finger fucked in my VW after the junior prom.) When I woke to his fingerings at 7:30, he stopped me when I slid down to blow him: "I don't feel comfortable with that."

Whether these strictures were psychotic "safe sex," or whether this was his way of staying half-true to his new husband I don't know. I only went ahead out of pragmatic horniness, thinking, whether or not we remain pals of any sort, I'll never stoop to sex with him again.

June 6, 1996

Home from the gym last evening, happily exhausted, reading the paper. The phone rings; it's Paul, whose postcard from Italy had just arrived, home again. "What're you doing tonight?"

"Waiting for you to come over and fuck," I said.

"I'll be over in an hour."

He looked real good when I went down to open the door; he has a sort of downcast, "aw, shucks" way of glancing up from his feet that's quite appealing—eerily reminiscent of 1980s bad-news boyfriend, Ray. We'd both had three weeks to think about what we'd done and might like to do when next given the chance. It was very nice setting aside my glasses and putting my arms around him and kissing like I meant it (I did). I felt awash in a sort of timelessness—

teary-eyed and cock-hard, greedy and bursting with joy at finding it: love.

"Let's just lie on the bed and kiss for a minute," I said, pulling him by the arm, believing this. "Then we'll sit on the couch and talk." But then we were hard and panting, and that was that for the evening. I felt incredibly turned on to him, to his specific body: hairy belly, funky crotch, red, very hard dick. He was talking some smutty sex talk—a thing I've always laughed at, but I wasn't laughing. We ended the second time around with him jerking off straddling my chest—"*Yeah, shoot in my face*"—and he did, turned-on and staring back at me as the warm drops hit my forehead, nose, mouth, and I came jerking myself.

June 10, 1996

Yesterday was another of those long, swell blossoming-of-romance days. Nice morning sex; we'd dressed to go out but started necking on the couch. I pulled off my T-shirt and shorts, leaving on jockeys and hightops; Paul sucked and batted around my hard-on through the cloth. We got back in bed. After some wrestling around dick-to-dick, he started putting fingers up my ass, slavering on the lube, working his way up to sticking his condom-sheathed cock in. Difficult at first, as usual, but then I was crouched and backing into him, jerking him off with my asshole and pumping at my own well-lubed cock, and I crossed the threshold about the time he began talking dirty about what he was doing, and I began telling him what I wanted (*"Yeah, all the way out and back in, slow..."*). He was fucking me the best I've ever had; I was aiming my ass at him trying to get it in at the best angle. Just as he pulled completely out, waited a beat, and shoved it brusquely back in, the yells of teenagers playing basketball in the court across the street wafted in on the hot breeze, like a gang cheering on a gang bang, and we both came, over-the-top with pleasure.

We cleaned up and drove to breakfast, then to the Castro for film festival tickets. We agreed on all our picks except for the three-hour B&W documentary on the elderly deaf Swedish lesbian World War II resistance fighters, but I decided I could always rent it later.

The day being clear and beautiful, we drove down Highway 1 to Gray Whale Beach; not until we were climbing down the hillside did I recognize it as the same beach Richard and I drove to in our first glow of meeting in September of '89, taking photos of each other naked—me sitting on a log, Richard walking into the waves.

We pulled off our clothes and lay on a sheet; I requested "The Paul Story," everything up till his moving to San Francisco. Not having brought sun block, we both got a bit burned, and my butt's doubly sore. Driving back to the city,

watching the blur of greenery spinning by alongside the freeway, hand in Paul's lap, sun streaming in the sun-roof, I had a
moment of pure happiness I couldn't have told without sobbing. I hadn't thought I'd get to have this again.

November 30, 1996 (Guerneville)
Yesterday, in the wake of Thursday's feasting, we drove up
Highway 1 to Fort Ross and walked up a trail past the Russian
cemetery, across the highway, and over a fire road to a deep
forest and stream. I came on to Paul, talking dirty and dick
hard, standing beside a toppled redwood, aroused by the forest, the mulchy leaf odor—remembering adolescent sex in the
woods at Fort Rucker. He'd expressed concern about being
caught when I'd hinted about it earlier—but after a glance or
two around, he pulled his dick out and I crouched and sucked
his swollen cock, very excited (memory of being unable to
breath during the penultimate scene of *Deliverance* sophomore
year)—pumping my own cock. I stood, and while he pinched
my nipples, I kissed him sloppily and jacked off, shooting onto
the mossy stones, and then he beat off while I stared and smut-
tily encouraged him till he shot. We kissed and held each other,
cold, noses wet, breathing hard, a little sunlight filtering down
through the trees.

We hiked back. Paul was for some reason jokily singing
the Barney song *("I love you, you love me…")* as we rounded

a bend in the leafy trail back nearer Sandy Cove and abruptly came upon a young couple and toddler sitting off the path on a blanket, the adults clinking glasses of wine—and we all laughed. A bit later we passed a group of older straight couples heading out. "Is it worth it?" one asked.

"Yes," I said.

About the author

Kevin Bentley's creative nonfiction has appeared in the *James White Review*, ZYZZYVA, *Diseased Pariah News*, *Flesh & the Word* 4 and 5, *His* 2, and *Bar Stories*. His work can also be found online at http://www.belief.net. Bentley wrote the text for *The Naked Heartland: The Itinerant Photographs of Bruce of LA*, and is the author of *Sailor: Vintage Photos of a Masculine Icon*. He is also the editor of *Afterwords: Real Sex from Gay Men's Diaries*.

Back cover photo: author,
Leavenworth & Geary rooftop, 1979